God is a Brown Girl Too

Cecilia B. Loving

Myrtle Tree Press LLC
Brooklyn, NY
www.myrtletreepress.webs.com

ISBN—978-0-9799247-2-9
ISBN—0-9799247-2-3
LCCN—2011923119

Book sales for North America and international:
Myrtle Tree Press LLC
376 President Street, Suite 2H
Brooklyn, New York 11231
Phone: 718-596-8019 (toll free 1-800-940-9642)
Fax: 888-583-7086; email orders to godisabrowngirltoo@gmail.com
Artwork created for God is a Brown Girl Too LLC
(www.godisabrowngirltoo.webs.com)
by Lawrence Hosannah

Printed in the United States of America

Dedication

For Brenda Cromwell and Nkiki Miller,

and Myrtle Lee, Essie Lee, Lena Mae, Jessie Mae, Hattie Mae, Fannie Mae, Dora Lee, Mazell, Julia, Mary, Joan, Sandra, Jewel, Raquiba, Liz, Cynthia, Cynthia Ann, Celeste, Ti'Sha, Di'Maya, Rahima, Belinda, Shirley, Louise, Carla, Christa, Camille, Bayliss, Dorothy, Fern, Taylor, Sandi, Kathleen, Angie, Andrea, Azalia, Avanti, Oprah, Michelle, Gay, Lia, Patricia, Marilyn, Robin, Paulette, Aakhu, Natalie, Judy, Judi, Celilianne, Tracey, Sheryl, Malena, Milena, Melissa, Myreah, Maya, Denise, Malesha, Farah, Cheryl, Allison, Jennifer, Betty, Cathy, Roberta, Julie, Paula, Bianca, Gail, Gayle, Esther, Laurie, Janice, Wendy, Ines, Elena, Christine, Christiana, Christina, Elizabeth, Naomi, Margo, Sara, Sarah, Sabrina, Stephanie, Ida, Clara, Lois, LaTanya, Beverly, Paige, Velma, Pamela, Dorothy, Iman, Yvonne, Yolanda, Marcella, Charlotte, Emma, Jocelyn, Shakira, Hillary, Rhonda, Pamela, Ashley, Amber, Joyce, Oza, Barbara, Alicia, Wanda, Eleanor, Sherie, Sherri, Dawn, Anu, Karen, Carol, Iyanla, Caryl, Priscilla, Renee, Renaye, Kim, Karmen, Mari, Martine, LaTeesha, Chrystal,

and every brown girl, of every conceivable root, every potential hue, and every dynamic blend...

from the God of every living breath that ever was and ever will be.

Contents

Prologue

This is not a story.

This is the truth.

This is how we glue the pieces back together that have fallen from our center of spiritual oneness. This is how we re-member ourselves. This is how we get back on our feet. This is how we believe again.

There are pieces, fragments, dreams, wishes, prayers of us all over the place—lights hidden under bushels, middle passages eroding the appearances of time and space. We need to find the legacies that were stolen from our lives. We need to move from the ordinary and reclaim the extraordinary in ourselves.

My mother was wise enough to tell me that I am God. I was wise enough to hear and even more precocious to believe her.

Jesus has appeared to me more than once. It took me years to understand why, but now I believe I have the gist of it, or at least I've learned how to move out of the way so that I can hear the Holy Spirit speak.

I've learned that God is not one color in particular or even a color at all. God is all colors, infinitely expressing as endless channels of cosmic vibrations. So I really hate it when we—many of us—really believe deep down inside that God is an old white man. If we cannot envision God as ourselves, then we are praying to someone we cannot reach. Jesus taught that God's kingdom is within us.

God is not a male or female or straight or gay. God is the divine energy giving endless expression to its image and likeness.

Therefore, no matter how society has tried to beat down the brown girl—as being less than or unworthy, God is most certainly a brown girl too. In fact, we were here first.

I heard the voice of God as a brown girl speaking. It is she who desired to write this book.

Sometimes she preaches. Sometimes she teaches. Sometimes she speaks through poetry. She also shares fragments of her scrolls of creation, evolution, freedom and victory. She was here before the Bible, so her story is different. More importantly, she is here now. She loves the Bible so she often quotes from scripture. She doesn't belong to any particular religion. She takes the liberty of being God to all cultures. While she is speaking, "I" move out of the way.

There's a bit of messiness and being unkempt to her voice because Absolute Good never shows up in a neat box. What you were looking for doesn't always come at a particular time, and things seldom turn out the way you anticipated. Some of our best lessons are often described as struggle or sin. Surprises are often tucked in the corners of unexpected disaster, and joy is sometimes mixed in with plain ole' foolishness. However, all you have to do is give your best, and realize the divine within.

Move From the Ordinary
and Reclaim
the Extraordinary

 જેન્જ

FROM HER SCROLL CALLED CREATION

*Love is forever and always was spectacular, audacious, free, and dark as the universe, dark as the vortex, dark as the horizon behind eyes staring up, dark as the beginning of all things
before shape was formed and light was named.
If you ask anyone who knows anything about Love, they will tell you in no uncertain terms that Love is God, or perhaps, they will say that God is Love.
But the truth is that Love cannot be contained inside of a word—
no matter how profound and eloquent.
Love cannot be contained inside of a word any more than God can be contained inside of a book.
Love is too all-encompassing to be bound and sold.*

*Love spreads herself every place that can be and will be, and wants to be and is. Love is unlimited source. Love is inexhaustible supply. Love is infinite support. Love is warm, smooth, and delicious. Love is laughter, smiles, grins. Love is energy from substance.
Love is magnet attraction and fulfillment.
Love is satisfaction, deliverance, and truth.*

*Inside Love is a song that we hear before our birth. Inside Love's song are our souls. Inside our souls, Love is present everywhere. Love has no obligation, and yet—to everything it is obligated. Love has no end, no conclusion, no shame, no remorse. Love is the only power that there is. Love is giver and gift, past and present, momentary and eternal, old and young, everywhere and nowhere,
the supreme activity of life that never fails.*

 જેન્જ

Re-Discover Your True Self

*When you know that I am you, and you are me—
you will begin to realize who God is.*

స్తు

Do you remember who I am? I am the Absolute Good that breathed you into being. I am the Divine Mind that gave you consciousness. I am the Endless Source that formed your soul. I am the Inexhaustible Supply that continues to feed you out of the eternal cosmos of the universe. Nothing came before me. I AM that I AM. I am the Creator here to remind you that my image and likeness is reflected as you. Creation is not something that happened and then stopped. Creation is something I did, and am still doing. Wherever there is creativity, there I am.

In order to know me in the Spirit, you will have to transcend the box of tradition in which you are locked. You will have to remove those strait-laced handcuffs of dependence, fear and shame. You will have to be bold enough to leave doctrine and diplomacy to embrace your own power. If you want to reclaim your life, acknowledging me—the Divine within—is not an option; it is a necessity. Men have so dominated your religion that most of you believe that I am an old white man.

Perhaps if you close your eyes and center your thoughts in a past that transcends the world as you know it, you can remember a creation that is older than European biblical tradition. Try to remember a beginning where ancient Africa was the Motherland of creation. Meditate on what Moses told the Israelites. He said "you forgot the God who gave you birth" (Deut. 32:18 NIV), or recall that Isaiah said God carried you since your birth (Isaiah 46:3). Imagine me from Hosea's perspective, who said that I taught you to walk, that I healed you, that I lifted you like a child to my cheek and bent down to feed you (Hosea 11:3-4).

I cannot be limited to words, but you may prefer to call me Spirit. Like "Love," Spirit is a term that you can use interchangeably with "God." The elusive sound of Spirit will help you stop picturing a person with a long white beard. Picture me as you growing in all directions at once. I am greater than you can imagine, comprised of everything that is. I am that point at which you find yourself. I am far greater than any pre-conceived notion of human sexuality or gender. If this is confusing, call me whatever you like. Call me "science" or "chance" or "coincidence" or "miracle." I am everything that is.

Throughout time, the bodies of women have carried and delivered my souls, those fragments of me from now to eternity. I am Alpha and Omega, the first and the last. These are my mountains and my valleys and my trees. This is my thunder and my rain and my river. You are all that I am. You cannot be limited, or minimized, or marginalized or demonized. You are my seed of life. Come and reclaim your rightful place as equal heirs to my throne.

True liberation of the oppressed, the imprisoned, the disenfranchised, the denigrated and the despised will only evolve as each individual evolves. It is up to each one of you to realize that you are more than your flesh, and to re-discover yourself as God. I am your liberation, your freedom through Spirit, and your connection to unconditional love. It is up to you to allow my light to glow in all of its magnificence as you. My beloved Jesus said "I am the Light of the world"—but also that you are the light of the world. Let your light shine.

Through you, I teach, nurse, build, draw, sell, purchase, divine, uplift, heal, nanny, negotiate, arbitrate, lawyer, doctor, sweep, mop, clean, cook, pray, baptize, massage, water, write, dance, model, sing, invent, farm, design, birth, pastor and encourage—not only the hearts of the privileged few but of the entire world. I fight for freedom. I abolish apartheid, genocide, lynch mobs, gas ovens, prostitution, slavery. I lead protests. I die for justice and equality. I go to jail in order to stand up for what I believe is right. I refuse to give up my seat. But I have not stopped killing and maiming and abusing and destroying because you have not. You have forgotten your true self worth. You have given up your power. You have yet to realize that you are my co-creator. You choose. You decide. You deliver. I can only do for you what I can do through you.

I send manna constantly, but you refuse to pick it up, or you still attempt to store it for yourselves. No matter how much you horde, you cannot be nurtured by it until you stop being afraid and be in my moment. You don't need to be greedy, or jealous, or spiteful—especially of one another. Imagine how foolish that looks to me, knowing that you have all that you need. I am your way out of no way, your Jesus on the main line, your calm in the storm, your gangster, your hook-up, your constant supply. Stop judging by mere appearances. Remember that you really are God.

⊰⊱

FROM HER SCROLL CALLED CREATION

Love breathed Grace into being,
and inside of her breath rose bones.
Love's breath stirred the bones, connecting them to her. Grace focused on
her breathing because she knew it was where she remembered love—
in her cells, in her energy, in her dreams.
She was before the light, wearing the divine darkness
as though it were her shroud.
She was empty and full, seamless yet connected, whole yet divided.
But she never knew that she was brown
because brown was all she ever knew.

Brown was the color of growing things, the color of her sister earth, the
color of beginnings, the color of the orbit from which all colors came and
blended with themselves. Brown was everywhere and at once without di-
mension or shape. Brown was without limit. Love manifested many beings
into physical form—in Love's image and likeness. But Grace was first.
She has the oldest bones and the oldest vibration
that ever danced from memory.

Step Into Your Greatness

When you stand on the edge of pure possibility,
you can use your prayer as the impetus to fly.

It is important for everyone to study and know the truth—especially you. Disregard those who believe that you have no right to God—for they want you to believe that you have no right to yourself. No woman or girl should be oppressed because of those who misinterpret the truth to mean that God is male and therefore, only men are God. I am inextricably part of each one of you in the same way that a breath is part of the wind. You, too, are the energy of life. There is no separation between all that I am and all that you are. Paul was right when he said that you live, move and have your being in God. You are my offspring (Acts 17:28).

All of you who see me in Jesus should be aware that Jesus acknowledged me in you when he said "I am in my Father, and you are in me, and I am in you" (John 14:20). Jesus said that the "kingdom of God is within you" (Luke 17:21). Jesus not only said I and the Father are One, he also said, "you are gods" (John 10:34). This is called oneness. This means that there is no separation between you and Spirit. This means that your greatness is waiting for you to express the Absolute Good that you are.

Feel me at the bottom of your feet. I am stepping through divine vibrations that I am sending from the tip of your toes up your muscles and bones—through your veins and glands—to the top of your head. I am always in your midst as your teacher, your companion and your guide. I always direct you, move you, lead you, speak to you, create through you, act through you, dance through you, and sing through you. I am always there, always here, always now.

I sing *"Jesus loves me this I know"* because it is Jesus whose teachings have taught many to step into their greatness. Jesus is the perfect manifestation of Spirit in creation. Jesus is the divine idea of God fully expressed as humanity. There is nothing like the blood of Jesus. But focus less on his crucifixion and more on his resurrection. Jesus has never stopped reminding Brown Girls everywhere that you will do "even greater things" than him (John 14:12). Eat those words with as much joy as you would a trip to Red Lobster, and let them slither off your tongue like those hot cheese biscuits.

Christ is not a person. Christ is the salvation, the stature that Jesus attained to show you that God dwells in all humanity. Paul said "Christ in you, the hope of glory" (Col. 1:27), teaching you that Spirit is your birthright.

I sing, *"Jesus on the main line, tell 'em what you want."* But Jesus does not merely teach you to ask for what you want. He commands that you do so—commands that you be in the right consciousness to receive it. Jesus is teaching you to step into the kingdom of God that is within you, and know that all else—every single detail of my good will be added to you (Matt. 6:31-33).

I sing *"Yes, Jesus loves me, yes, Jesus loves me"* because Jesus taught you that if you don't have the good sense to ask in your own name, ask in his. He said that he will serve as your proxy and your healer and your friend. But he taught you these things so that eventually you would become wise enough to touch the hem of your own garment. There is fish and bread for you to multiply. There are oceans for you to walk. There are dead among you who need to be raised. There are stones that need to be redeemed from accusers. There are wellsprings of living water to drink. But I need you to stand up my daughter—in a consciousness that realizes you have whatever it takes. You will never be successful if you do not grasp the unlimited power that I am as you. I don't care about your weave, your Gucci, your rock or the glitter of your rims—even your millions don't matter. Only when you awaken to your true self do you step into your greatness.

֎֎

FROM HER SCROLL CALLED CREATION

*Created before words, or stories, or clothing, or dreams, Grace knew that
she was Spirit expressed as bones and flesh, as well as she knew her
breath, as well as she knew her heart, as well as she knew the long warmth
growing out of her head, brown and dusty twists of roots, vines, and cords
inextricably intertwined, twisted, centered, corn-rowed and connected to
divine vibration. There was no pretense, she simply was. There was no
foolishness, or reluctance, or shame to being the God that Love breathed
into her, the breath of Spirit, infused with the power to co-create, blessed
with the ability to enlighten, shape, color, extend, swarm, express, be.*

*Being God and being Brown, to her, was synonymous. God is what Love
breathed into all of her children: children of endless creation crawl, caress,
climb, soar, deliver. God reminded them that they were each special, and
yet—they were one. There really was no separation, for out of the same
seed they came, were born, lived and surrendered to the divine darkness
of all they ever were.*
Hush!
When Love speaks, it's like a dream.
Listen.

֎֎

Listen to Me

Move beyond the sound where your voice asks God,
and go to the space where your soul listens.

ॐ◈

Beloved, do you know the importance of stillness? Do you know the importance of being quiet? Do you know the importance of listening to the Universe present in and as you? If you listen, you can always hear me, you can always hear the kingdom of God within. Do you understand the importance of that *something* moving you from within? Does *something* ever tell you to go in a particular direction? Does *something* ever tell you to call a particular person? Does *something* ever tell you to read a book that falls right off the shelf into your hands? Does *something* ever tell you to fix a situation that you know has long been in need of fixing?

How often have you failed to listen to that still, small voice in your head, or that nagging feeling in your gut, or that anticipation in your heart, or that energy in your soul? That *something* was with you ever since you were born, guiding you and directing you as long as you practiced an awareness of it. Perhaps you discovered this *something* accidentally when you began writing poetry at twelve, realizing that words flowed from *something* through you like a stream vibrating with color and smell and taste and feeling. Perhaps this *something* reminded you that it was there when you first began to dance and it filled your limbs with a passion and joy beyond this world. Perhaps this *something* delivered you through the voice that it spoke within you, expressing itself dramatically, compassionately, and wonderfully as being.

Perhaps you finally became courageous enough to call this *something*—this still small voice, this creative energy, this glorious movement, this call to be one with life itself—"Spirit." Spirit, yes I, have always been part of you, always been there at the point at which you recognized your oneness with the Universe.

I AM the breath of life—always speaking, always guiding, always directing.

I was always here—long before Joel prophesized (Joel 2:28). I was here long before Jesus told you that: "the Counselor, the Holy Spirit, whom the Father will send in my name, will teach you all things, and remind you of everything I have said to you" (John 14:26). He said that when "the Spirit of truth comes, he will guide you into all the truth" (John 16:13). But I was here before the beginning of time. The day of Pentecost is a day that you need to keep re-living until you realize that we are one. You sometimes need violent winds to fill a place. You sometimes need to speak in tongues. You sometimes need lightening to flash and trumpets to sound in order to know that you are *filled with the Holy Spirit* (Acts 2: 1-4). But I was always here with you—that *something* calling you to fulfill life's divine appointment.

I urge you to get off the phone, to stop reading email, to turn off the television, to get off Facebook, to stop texting your friends, to stop surfing the net. YouTube will always be there. The only way that you can center in the silence for 15 minutes (or however long you can take to be still) is to turn off your distractions. I am always speaking. All you have to do is be quiet enough to listen. If you do, you will hear me speaking as that *something* within. I will guide you and bless you beyond your imagination.

When Jesus said "blessed are your eyes, for they see, and your ears, for they hear," he meant your inner ear, your contemplative mind, your open heart. Isaiah told you that "Whether you turn to the right or to the left, your ears will hear a word behind you saying, 'This is the way, walk in it'" (Isaiah 30:21).

Listen.

ॐॐ

§

FROM HER SCROLL CALLED CREATION

*Dark Brown is the color of peace—easily accessed behind shut eyes,
secret places, inner chambers, quiet space. Dark Brown is the true color of
spiritual illumination. Dark Brown is the lens through which she opened
her third eye into universes of infinite music singing to itself. Dark Brown
is the color of divine ideas stretching toward the birth canal of endless possibilities. It was in Love's consciousness of endless creation
that Grace first spoke things into being.
Let there be Wind. Let there be Rain.
Let there be Light.
Let there be souls who suck at the divine breast of endless creation and
feed from the fountain of eternal wisdom.*

*Are you kidding? She never ate forbidden fruit, or lusted at the beckon of
serpents. Snakes did not speak because the world communicated through
the rhythmic beat of the universal Love. Grace moved easily through the
garden of the world, commanding all the creatures as she deposited some
fragment of her imagination, some gems, some tiny grains of sand—to be
multiplied and then, blessed. Her feet never tired of strolling through the
meadows of fresh, rhythm, silence, grass. The scarlet butterflies and the
golden winged birds and the long-necked giraffes and the rambunctious
elephants also multiplied and created. Grace created movement and then
she moved, dancing and then she danced, leaping and then she leaped—
over oceans and seas and lakes formed from her sweat.*

§

Find Your Place in My Kingdom

The Buddhists ask do you remember the face of your parents before you were born? The Brown Girl answers "Yes, it was my own. The face of the universe without boundaries. The face of miracles through the centuries. The face of butterflies resurrecting from heaven. The face of God shouting 'Hallelujah.'"

ಹ⊷ಳ

In order to seek the kingdom of God, you need to know that it is not in the hereafter, it is in the now. Seeking the kingdom is a metaphor for your awareness of the presence, power and wisdom of God as yourself. The kingdom is closer to you than your hands and feet. You are God's temple and God's Spirit lives in you. (1 Cor. 3:16). Find the place in you where the kingdom of God lives. Jesus said "I am in my Father, and you are in me, and I am in you" (John 14:20). Find the presence of Jesus in you. It can be as small or as large as you like. It can dwell in you or you in it. In the kingdom of God, you will re-discover me, and will once again feel the love of the universe as something good that never stops giving.

By seeking the kingdom of God first, you will be moved in the direction of your dreams. Imagine it for yourself—like a Garden of Eden, a connection with endless source that gives whenever you need it. As soon as you ask, you will receive. When you know that it is my pleasure to give you the kingdom, you will feel your cup running over and the abundance of good that pours and flows from it. You will experience true abundance in that moment that you know me for yourself.

When you really know *that you know that you know*—that you have the power of the Almighty God within you, then you will be at the top of your game. If you trust Spirit to guide you to the Truth, then all of the opportunities that you need will present themselves to you; all of the resources that you need will become available to you; all of the teachers that you need will show up as your guide. My kingdom is always in your midst, always embracing you with its riches—not by luck or chance—but by my law. Divine law is always kept.

ॐ৯

FROM HER SCROLL CALLED CREATION

She was whatever she imagined—
muscular or fat, tiny or weak, curvaceous or strong.
She created the world through dark brown eyes
and smiled at it with perfect teeth
and smelled it with pronounced nostrils.
Her brown arms fearlessly swam the blue waves of love's creation. She was
all that beauty was in Love's eternal way. Love adorned Grace as a per-
fect expression. She was given the power to look like whatever she chose to
create—be it cliff diver, mountain climber or agile runner. No matter how
she chose to manifest herself, she always expressed Love, the pure substance
of all life, a movement, a rhythm,
a vision part of and unfolding through everything.

ॐ৯

Shine Your Light

Dance with the grace of even greater things.
Speak with the words that summon change.
Pray with the light that ignites your faith.
Dare to be born in the consciousness of Christ.

෨৵৽

You believe that you are just flesh and bones, but you are not. You are a being of light. When you are tapped in and turned on to me, perfect health and wholeness radiates from all of your pores. The right people and information flow magically towards you while I light the way. This is what some people call "perfect divine order." It will place you at your appointed time, in your right place, doing what you are supposed to do, when you are supposed to be doing it.

When you need to get your glow on, I am the only real exfoliate. Not only do I clean the toxins from your body, but I scrub away the thoughts that clog your mind—and I do it all for free. All you have to do is get rid of anything blocking my flow. I clear warts, acne, rashes, fungus, and infections. All you have to do is tap my inexhaustible supply, my healing presence, and my divine wisdom. Focus on the thoughts that you think, the words that you use, and how you treat your sisters and brothers. You can have the most pristine diet and exercise plan, but if you have unclean thoughts, words or deeds, you will still lack the type of true illumination that will radiate throughout your entire being.

In Mark 7:15, Jesus said "Nothing outside a man can make him 'unclean' by going into him. Rather, it is what comes out of a man that *makes* him 'unclean.'" He said in Mark 7:18-22 that out of your hearts, come evil thoughts, theft, murder, adultery, greed, malice, deceit, lewdness, envy, slander, arrogance and folly. It is only when you release your filthy thoughts and have a clean heart, that you have an enlightened soul.

You begin the process of spiritual exfoliation when you stop wallowing in the discord of your bad vibrations. You create a clean heart when you stop enjoying self-pity and start enjoying self-love. You create a clean heart when you stop using your energy to denounce someone and instead use your energy to lift them up. You create a clean heart when you stop believing that the only way to attract your good is to interfere with something belonging to someone else. You create a clean heart when you are confident that I will bless you just like I bless everyone else.

You can't sneak around on the outside and pretend that you're clean on the inside. You can't lie to people and pretend that you have your act together. You can't try to get over on somebody and pretend that you mean them well. You can't stop short of giving all of the good that you are. A deep, penetrating cleanser of the soul always reveals that you must take the high road regardless of the situation.

Taking the high road means that even when others are wrong, you forgive them. Forgiveness is fundamental to releasing the inner light. Forgiveness releases inner toxins and cleanses regret, which is essential to the exfoliation process. Forgiveness requires completion. Whatever you let go should remain released. You wouldn't pick up any sloughed off skin cells, so you certainly wouldn't want to recycle any toxic emotions, or relationships, or memories of any sort. Release them, and let go of them, and never look back. When you keep dipping into the past, you never move forward, and thus completely dim the light of the new day shining as you.

A gritty, penetrating soul exfoliation may even require more focused help from me. I am always available to penetrate those uneven patches, or troublesome blotches, or ashy dry spots of consciousness. Whenever you cannot reach into the wayward corners of your existence and pull out all of your pain, I am here to do it for you. The Psalmist says, in the 51st Psalm, the 10th through the 12th verses, "Create in me a pure heart, O God; and renew a steadfast spirit within me. Do not cast me from your presence or take your Holy Spirit from me. Restore to me the joy of your salvation and grant me a willing spirit, to sustain me." In other words, you don't have to do it alone. I will help you scrub off the doubt; scrape off the fear; strip away the envy; and clean up the deceit when you are ready to admit that you can't do it alone. Once you allow me to help you, you will be amazed at how fast I work.

I can transform the people, places and circumstances in your life so fast that you will be astounded. All you have to do is bless the changes—bless the people I remove, bless the situations that I change, bless the new channels that I open. Don't try to hold onto anyone or anything. If you do, you will only stagnate your growth. Look at Lot's wife, she turned into a pillar of salt just by looking back.

The radiance of my light will shine from the changes that you grow through because they are doors opening my infinite channels of Good. When you are open and receptive to change, you give way to the best in you. Clean out the useless, the toxic and the blockage so I can fill your cleared spaces with something more spectacular. Let go of the old so that I can bless you with the new. The right people, events and circumstances will flow to you with ease when you are open and receptive. When your past is released and your baggage is discarded, your entire being will glow with a new radiance. Only then can the fullness of my love shine through you.

෨ஜ

FROM HER SCROLL CALLED CREATION

Grace knew that none of Love's expressions have limitations; all are full of infinite possibilities and pure potential. Grace knew to listen, love, breathe, be, create. Grace knew to open the eyes of all souls—to all that they are capable of, all of which defies the logic of what can be seen with the naked eye. Grace knew whoever planted lies would perish at the hand of their own foolishness. There was nothing woolly, nappy, odd, or goblin-like about Grace's appearance. She was not a heathen nor the size of a small boy who liked to climb trees. She was grander and more majestic than any woman ever known to humanity—wrapped in soft dreadlocks, twists, braids, roots, and twines in Love's arms. She was beautiful not bewildered. She smiled deeply, never grinned. She commanded firmly, never scolded. She praised strenuously, never condemned.

Walk in Your Light

Wherever you are when you are ready to shine your light,
you will find the Promised Land.
No matter how long it takes for you to reach it,
it will always be there.

☙❧

Your light is your legacy. It is so inseparable from you that you are obligated to let it shine. In Matthew 5:14-15, Jesus said: "You are the light of the world. A city on a hill cannot be hidden. Neither do people light a candle and put it under a bowl. Instead they put it on its stand, and it gives light to everyone in the house. In the same way, let your light shine before men that they may see your good deeds." You cannot pick and choose who will benefit from your light. You must be generous enough to share it with everyone. How? By simply doing what I have called you to do—walk in your light, walk in your purpose, and walk in your calling. Do what you love to do, what you do best, what harms no one else—and the joy that you give will be beyond your comprehension. Sharing your gifts and talents has a viral effect that will flow through the universe and bless millions for ages to come.

What you don't realize is that even after you make your transition from this life, your light will still shine so brightly that it will lead people everywhere. Paul told the Ephesians (5:8), to walk as children of Light. Walk in obedience to Spirit. Walk in the beauty of discipline. Walk in the power of faith.

Walk beyond the confines of your self-imposed limitations, so that I can shine through you. Walk as an unlimited expression of all that I AM. You cannot judge your gifts and talents. You cannot see the fullness and wholeness that you contribute to the Universe simply by being the best that you are. Don't lose your way because of what other people say or do or think. You are uniquely you for a reason. The lack of support, criticism or condemnation by some of my other children is like the wind. It is as fleeting as a single breath. Don't be fooled by cowards and haters to be a second-rate you. You are more than a diva, you are the divine. Walk in the beauty of your light. Otherwise, you will never give me the life that you have promised me in the Spirit, and the Promised Land will always be a distant reality.

Your greatest achievements began as divine ideas that no one else believed in. Jesus said (Matthew 25:34), "Come, you who are blessed by my Father; take your inheritance, the kingdom prepared for you since the creation of the world." Come you who no longer care what others think. Come you who are no longer afraid to move forward into the greatness that you are. Come you who believe in the magnificence of Spirit. Come you who have brought oil for your lamp and are willing to let your light shine through. Come all ye faithful. Come ye, O' come ye to Bethlehem—that house of bread, that place of substance, that center of Truth. O' come Beloved, from the far country, and behold the Christ within. O' come Spiritual Rebirth, come with the Light of a new day. O' come embrace the power that you were given, the true gift of transformation, the joyous deliverance that you can attain through a consciousness of Spirit.

You were called before your birth. The Buddhists ask "do you remember what your face looked like before your parents were born?" Jeremiah said before we were formed in the womb, God knew us. Before we were born, God set us apart (Jeremiah 1:4-6). You may not remember exactly where you are going or know how you will get there, but I will lead the way. I will give you the voice and the vision and the victory that you need. I will part the Red Sea so that no one will deter you from your path.

As I told the Psalmist, "Do not touch my anointed ones; do my prophets no harm" (Psalm 105:15). Just stay on the path, as Denzel Washington said in *The Book of Eli*. Stay on the path of righteousness, regardless of evildoers. Return from the far country. Go on about my business. Don't just get a glimpse of the Promised Land, but be in the right consciousness to enter it. Be a believer—not just in somebody else's testimony, but know me for you. Shut up and listen to Spirit for yourself. Be liberated in the unlimited power of all that you are. Walk the walk and talk the talk—with the sword of my power. Watch a thousand fall at your side and ten thousand fall at your right hand and nothing come near you (Psalm 91:7).

This reminds me of the Israelites who were at the edge of the wilderness, when Moses blessed them as they journeyed into the Promised Land. They were not just standing on the bank of a river to cross. They were on the threshold of a new consciousness. They were not just leaving the wilderness because they had traveled a certain distance, or mapped out a particular strategy, or had served a certain amount of time. They were crossing over because they were ready.

The Promised Land is not a physical place. It is a place in consciousness that gives you spiritual food that feeds your mind, soul and heart, the unlimited feast of my Kingdom. It is a place where you will no longer be captive to the wilderness of your own negativity, grumbling and strife. It is a place where materialism and greed will no longer enslave you. But you cannot get there until you are ready.

The number forty in the Bible symbolizes preparation rather than a specific number. Forty years in the wilderness means as long as it takes to get ready. You are ready when you realize that I AM always working with you for your greatest good. I will always feed you enough manna—enough *spiritual* food to sustain you. You are ready when you stop worrying about what other people say or think. As Terrie Cole Whitaker says, *What You Think About Me is*

None of My Business. You are ready when you are willing to make the sacrifices that need to be made to accomplish what you want. You are ready when you learn that I AM within.

You are ready when you can bless even the appearances of life—whether they are bad or good—because you realize that they are the motivation that you need. You are ready when you understand that love is the spiritual law that supersedes all others. Love does not judge but is unconditional. Love has an all-encompassing heart that fulfills Karma with Grace. You can accomplish anything with the power of love. If you are worried or doubtful or in need, all you have to do is bless the situation with the power of love. Love is my energy in its most powerful form. Love allows you to be compassionate toward everyone, even when they second-guess you, because you know that they are part of your blessing. Even when others mean something for evil, I mean it for good (Genesis 50:20). They serve as the catalyst that pushes you beyond your comfort zone and make you aim higher than you ever aimed before.

You cross over to the other side when you know that you are blessed with my anointing. You never know how you are going to make it there. But you can trust that I will put the right people on your path to push against your resistance and pull you across the threshold to something better and greater.

You have spent enough time in the wilderness. You are ready to do what I have called you to do—ready to walk in the newness of life, and nothing and no one can stop you.

FROM HER SCROLL CALLED CREATION

If you have walked by faith and not by sight—believed in things hoped for but never seen; if you have known God, known Jesus Christ, known the Holy Spirit, known Allah, known Jehovah, known Buddha, known Krishna, known Ra, known Vishnu, known Rama, known Waheguru, known Yahweh, known omnipotence by any name—then you have known Grace.

If you have stretched forth, if you have taken the limits off, if you have removed the boundaries, if you have manifested increase, if you have been released from fear, from doubt, from trepidation—from whatever is holding you back, and moved forward into a new existence—elevated on a new plane, then you have known Grace.

If you prayed for an answer then surrendered to faith; if you doubted in the head but never in the heart; if you had nothing in the world except a simple prayer that you were being blessed then and there, then you have known Grace—always blessing, renewing, painting, recreating in countless planets, spheres, realms, galaxies, universes, cosmos.

This was the beginning.

I can speak of it, in fragments, in pieces of dead scrolls, in secrets pulled from under rocks, in bottles tossed to the sea—because I know.
These are my bones.

Receive the Riches of My Universe

Open your heart carefully.
Step inside your endless possibilities.
Taste a fragment of your divine ideas.
Walk the waters of your conviction.
Stop at nothing short of your own magic,
your own miracles,
your own recognition of Spirit's
inexhaustible source.

৵৽

Many of you, who are on the religious rather than the spiritual path, refrain from a candid discussion of prosperity. The irony is that you condemn those who claim the kingdom as rightful heirs; you wallow in dismay at the economy, massive lay-offs, soaring oil prices, mortgage insanity and other appearances of lack; and yet you have the gall to beg others to give you what you have the power to create for yourself. You live in an environment where some of your sisters and brothers are billionaires, some hit the lottery for millions, and yet some cannot seem to make ends meet. But you still ridicule your ability to manifest what you want when you want it.

Jesus said don't worry about what you shall eat or drink or wear because I know that you have need of these things. Jesus is saying that if you are in the right consciousness, which is one of receptivity to the flow of infinite good, you cannot help but attract riches of the universe—regardless of the appearances around you. I want the best for you. I am always waiting to multiply your fish and bread. I am always waiting to heal your affliction.

I will say this again. You are heirs to my throne. You will do even greater works than Jesus. You always have the power to ask and receive; seek and find; knock and know that the door will be opened.

છે.

Each one of you is unique seed, endowed with the power to attract what and who you need for your growth. Each one of you has the power of choice in a universe abundant with divine ideas. You have the power to choose a consciousness of abundance, one in which you can manifest the good that you desire. Alternatively, you can choose to dwell in a state of cynicism, skepticism and doubt—meeting every ray of sun with a dark cloud, so apprehensive and resistant to my presence that day seems like night. Choose the path that you want to take.

I am telling you Beloved to take the path of the good seed. The path of the good seed is not the one where you are scattered to the wind, or unable to deepen your roots and grow, but one where you are receptive to me—open and aware of my inexhaustible source and endless supply. Each one of you have the ability to use your power of creative choice to plant divine ideas, to sow them with love, to grow them with faith, and to reap a bountiful harvest of success. When you do, you will learn that the most critical time in the manifestation of your dreams is the time during which you cannot see your desires take root and grow.

You enjoy seeing evidence, signs of growth. When you don't, you throw in the towel and decide that nothing is happening. You tell yourself that I have forgotten you. You imagine that everyone is plotting against you. It seems like there are unnecessary delays, unwarranted obstacles and unjustified quicksand where you appear to get stuck. But what is really happening is that you are growing in consciousness and the expansion of your growth roots you solidly in faith—formed from a strong foundation in me. Before long, you begin to see that the obstacles, the challenges, the appearances of discord were merely opportunities to grow in love, strength, power, wholeness.

If you could just see the beauty of your life transforming, you would never hesitate; you would never doubt; you would just bless each tight squeeze, each pull in another direction, each so-called setback, each surprise twist. Despite your frustration, life is never a completely linear process. When you stay the course, you will have your season. One day, when you least expect it, all your sowing will bring blessings that will come pouring, rushing, streaming, flowing in. You will find yourself gloriously in bloom—your prayers answered and your dreams manifested. You will experience the harvest of your faith.

The book of James, Chapter 1, Verse 4, says, "Perseverance must finish its work so that you may be mature and complete, not lacking anything." The path of the good seed unfolds a process that is just as wonderful as its end result. It is a process that simply cannot be crowded in one instant. Just pull back your hair, put on your cap, get your umbrella—or do whatever you must do in order to enjoy your season of trials and tribulations—however it shows up. You can weather the storm.

You cannot see it, but you are part of a divine plan unfolding all that you have planted. It is only when you keep the faith that you see your good unfolding like the lotus of countless petals—more magnificent, more joyful, more awesome than you could ever imagine.

ॐॐ

Genesis, which means to initiate, teaches you that you can plan your good and bring it into manifestation by decreeing it. It is as simple as knowing what you desire and speaking it into existence through the divine substance that is always in your midst. Whatever you need for the manifestation of your dreams is drawn to you through my spiritual gravity—me seeking you through your desires. When you have clarity about what you want in your life, it manifests quickly. Be careful what you ask for because you will get it.

When you are certain about what you want to accomplish—visualize it, write it out, affirm it, and move swiftly towards its manifestation. No person, no situation, no circumstance can keep your good from you. Nothing is lost. No time is lost. No money is lost. No opportunity is lost. I will restore what you claim is missing. As I said to Abraham, "lift up your eyes and look from where you are—northward and southward and eastward and westward—for all the land that you see, I will give to you."

The story of Abraham demonstrates a divine plan in process. I was telling Abraham to use his vision to imagine my Good—as far as his eyes could see. When co-creating your divine plan, don't underestimate my ability to bless you. Visualize whatever you want in your life, then be receptive to me manifesting even more: say "God, if not this, then something better."

You have an open door, which no one can shut. You have unlimited power. All you need to do is claim it. All you need to do is co-create your divine plan with faith. The divine plan is the power of your words constantly creating by their decree; the ability to envision your good before it even takes shape; and the persistence to not let go until you are blessed by the infinite, unlimited flow of good that is sitting in the universe—just waiting for you to claim it.

❧⥤

You know that the Book of Exodus, the story about how God used Moses to free the Israelites from bondage in Egypt, is about liberation. But you always focus on it from the perspective of liberation of the body rather than liberation of the mind. In order to create what you desire, you have to liberate your consciousness too. Exodus teaches you that Moses was directed by God to demonstrate a number of plagues to force Pharaoh to free the Israelites. Yet, the Israelites also had to let go of Pharaoh. They had to get rid of their slave mentality. When Pharaoh finally let the Israelites go, I led them on a 'round about way' through the wilderness because I knew that even though they were destined for the Promised Land, if they took a short cut, they would also have a short cut back to Egypt. I wanted to make it difficult for them to hang on to the past.

This is not really different from your own life. Even though you are free, you find yourself in bondage to experiences in the past or to worries about the future—neither of which is taking place in the now. This mental bondage is what blocks you from greater accomplishments. The Israelites were in bondage to an existence in which they relied on others to take care of their needs. They complained to Moses, saying what have you done to us by bringing us out of Egypt? It would have been better for us to serve the Egyptians than to die in the desert. In response, Moses preached to the Israelites to stand firm and trust in me. Moses tried to get them to stop depending on a consciousness that did not serve them. The only way that they could create a consciousness of faith was by cleansing and releasing the past. Moses led his people through the waters of the Red Sea, enabling them to cleanse their consciousness and release their shackles of dependence on others rather than on Divine Source.

The Red Sea is a metaphor symbolizing parting from the old and accepting the new. If you take the first step out of the land of captivity, you will find your Red Sea parting. If you truly believe in me as the unlimited power of Divine Source always available to you, you will let go of fear and accept my guidance. If you really trust in the power within, you will walk through the Red Sea of your consciousness with a pure heart and a liberated mind, and witness your obstacles fall away and the gates to your Promised Land opening.

෴

What better demonstration of my inexhaustible supply than the First Book of Kings, the 17th Chapter, when the Prophet Elijah went to Zarephath and asked a starving widow for food. Even though the widow only had a handful of flour in a jar and a little oil in a jug, she shared what she had with Elijah. After she gave, they had food everyday—and the flour was not used up, nor did the jug of oil run dry. When we give what we have without attachment, we are always blessed.

What you give always returns, not because you are looking for something. Your good might not appear to be returned from the same source, but all substance is the same—poured through many channels. The good news is that when your gifts return, they will be multiplied many times over. In Malachi 3:7, I said, "Return to me, and I will return to you. Bring the whole tithe into the storehouse, that there may be food in my house. Test me in this, and see if I will not throw open the floodgates of heaven and pour out so many blessings that you will not have room enough to receive them (Malachi 3:10). Giving is not merely an act, it is a state of consciousness.

When you give freely, you open your heart to accept the free-flowing abundance of the universe. You allow God's Good to bless you by releasing any belief of lack. As Paul said to the Corinthians, "Whoever sows sparingly will also reap sparingly, and whoever sows generously will also reap generously." So if you want love, give the love that you want. If you want peace, be the peace that you desire. If you want joy, stir up the joy that you expect. No matter what it is, if it is good—give it, knowing that it will return. Give way to a new consciousness, allowing me to give back to you whatever you ask. Move out of your way and allow my abundance to pour out so many blessings that you will not have room enough to receive them.

☙❧

ॐॐ
FROM HER SCROLL CALLED EVOLUTION

mama covered the earth as dark as her brown girls—first grace, then
myrtle, then acacia, through generations to mary, devi, desire, victory,
harriet, paulette,mari, trisha, aum, strong and sweet and wise—made in
the image of their mother.
the way she formed the substance of all things
breathing life to creation, listening to prayers,
building a universe inside the space of an atom
in a continuum of energy
that has no time except the present.
to call that the future
she nods as if it were yesterday
when her children were the moons and stars and suns—
flickering in the eyes,
dancing in the beat of her wayward sons
(how she wept over their constant fighting)
in enoch, babel, ninevah, rwanda, dakar, iraq.
sons sinning for power,
who do not remember the ark,
or egypt, or canaan, or golgotha.
sons ever so often returning home,
begging for forgiveness,
as if their penance would actually give them
the sanctity of peace, crying as if mama
would always grant them a miracle.
she, the eye of eternity,
cannot even remember herself—what she looks like
and why she keeps answering them,
even when they call her
"Father."

ॐॐ

Leap and I Will Catch You

You are the breath of the wind.
Your freedom is inside your soul.
You leap in and out of spaces
wearing the songs of endless creations.
You cannot be measured, defined or contained.
Your season is here.

৵৵

You are enough—right where you are. You are beautiful enough. You are rich enough. You are creative enough. You are wise enough. You are good enough. You don't have to find your so-called "soul mate": I AM your soul mate. Nothing in the external world completes you. Your job doesn't complete you. It is but one of many paths to give and grow in consciousness. Your cars don't complete you. Your clothes, bags, shoes don't complete you. Your titles don't complete you, nor do the degrees, nor do the trophies of life that you collect. When you let go of all of the stuff that you use to validate who you are, you will begin to see that your mission, your calling, your deepest desire will always be enough to sustain you. All you have to do is leap, and I will be there to catch you.

I AM your season. I am not based on the economy. Quit shaking from the illusion of instability. I am the only stable force that there is. Release the material, and be courageous enough to recreate your life with a new consciousness. You are emerging from old wine skins simply because they can no longer contain you. You are new wine.

Your new wine is bold, unrestricted, imaginative and daring enough to walk, dance, step, leap beyond the person that you thought you were to express—to the infinite possibility that I AM calling you to be. You have not yet begun to taste the joy that my

Spirit is blessing you with, the good that I long to unfold through you.

Your new wine pushes you outside of complacency—to unfold a new vision—one that no longer compares you to others but realizes that I made each one of you wonderful, unique beings, blessed with the abundance of inexhaustible supply.

This is your season. I am calling you to let go of everything and everyone, to leave the mediocre, the mundane and the material, and to stand fully and completely as you are—aware of your greatness. When you are in tune to me expressing as you, you will find yourself above the fray. Your gifts and talents will be expressed in greater ways than you can yet imagine. You will give more. You will be better. You will know that you are one with a power that is stronger than anything in the physical realm. This awareness is the only thing that you need for wings to soar to heights thought unreachable.

Even if you feel pressed, pushed against the wall, blinded by the debt of defeat, now is not the time to fear, worry or wallow. Now is the time to be the children of God, the heirs to the throne, the greatness that you are. Now is the time to know within every aspect of your being that you are made in my image and likeness, and that right where you are standing is holy ground.

Right in your soul is a love without boundaries, a love that beckons you to experience who you really are instead of who you used to be.

You may be forced to discard old jobs, old conditions, old circumstances, old relationships, old places, old doubts. But your release of the old is merely allowing you to take a leap to new heights.

You don't need a big space to take off from. All you need is the space in your heart to trust that I am not just inside of your prayers. I am inside of all that is—appearing in the vortex of your clasped hands. I am the air. I am the sky. I am your wings.

All you have to do is leap, and I will carry you the rest of the way.

ॐ

FROM HER SCROLL CALLED CREATION

Karma and Grace looked just alike, except for hair and skin—if you don't really count the fact that Grace was nearly a foot taller. They were the first women, and they were brown. Grace's brown hair was thick and long like the roots and vines that she loved, with a hint of red clay earth and sun blonde radiance; and her skin was the dark color of ground cinnamon.

Karma's hair was full as a lion's mane, wavy, black, majestic—almost self-righteous; and her skin was the color of sand,
the color of a smooth tan stone.
They were almost exact opposites.
They rarely fought—except the time that Karma struck Grace
for being too perfect.

"You're being silly," Grace said. "We were both made in God's image and likeness so how could either one of us be more or less." Yet, Karma—feeling her own sense of inadequacy attacked Grace again.
This time, Love separated them into different parts of the hemisphere.
Grace was content to stay alone in the world because she had already spent time doing so,
but Karma was afraid.

Some say it was her fear of being alone that cause her to split in half.
Some say it was Love. Love divided her into two parts, to show her that a couple are always two parts of a whole and also that everything you need is always within.

ॐ

Awaken to Love

ରେ ଏବି

FROM HER SCROLL CALLED CREATION

Karma's partner Mandla was that part of her that was intellectual and strong, yet sensuous and sweet. He wasn't judgmental like her at all. He was playful, mischievous, funny. He would wallow in the excitement of movement and magic and stars. He would paint and frolic and re-create. He was always tearing down things and fixing them again. He did not have the benefit of spending eons with the before, but once he felt the early morning sun across his deep brown face—he could remember everything about love that Karma could—because they were one.

Mandla liked to soar with birds, swim with whales, rest beneath clouds— always yearning for adventure. When Mandla traveled, Karma missed him—his deep dark skin the color of earth, thick black hair, his full sumptuous lips. It was a time when men and women were not separate as we know them today. They did not look to each for love; they realized that love was who they were. They could summon each other with their hearts. It was unbridled ecstasy—without fear.

They were so wonderful together that Love divided them into new souls. And those souls gave way to new souls. And those bones gave way to new bones. And that flesh gave way to new flesh. And yet, they were all part of the same Spirit. Generations were born from their union who understood their karmic fate in the physical. Their souls were all expressions of Love.

ରେ ଏବି

My Love is Here

This is the time for your own magic.

ॐ∽ॐ

There is nothing that I hate more than seeing my daughters fight over men. There is nothing that makes you more dishonest, disrespectful, disloyal and deceptive than when you are afraid that you will not find that half of you that you jokingly call "better." Beloved, you are trying to find the right one but he is looking for you. Proverbs 18:22 says "He who finds a wife finds what is good thing and receives favor"; it doesn't say "she" who finds a man. You've got it twisted. You insist on degrading yourselves, belittling yourselves, referring to yourselves as nappy-headed bitches and hos, calling yourselves pimps, and attacking one another. The reason that your soul mate cannot find you is because he cannot recognize you. When he called your name in the spiritual ethers, something else answered—and it wasn't you—at least not the real you. You are your own magic. You are your own love—ceaseless with giving. If you can no longer see your beauty and all that you bring, just see my love. My love is here. My love will restore the real you.

When you open your eyes in the morning, the first thing you should think about is not how to get your groove on, but how to be a love that transcends sex. Think about the love in which you live and move and have your being. Think about the love that created the universe and is constantly co-creating through you. Think about the love in whose image and likeness you were born. My daughters didn't give birth to any bitches. Quit pretending that you are less than your true worth. Quit trying to play the universe with false bravado. I'm not going to give you any more than you are willing to believe. Now is not the time to lose yourself in internet fantasies, television reality shows, endless text messages, Facebook posts, overpriced shoes or baby daddy drama. Now is the time for your own magic.

If you try, you can feel my love anointing you with each second of my breath. You can hear my love sung in empty spaces of your own silence. You can see my love caressing the brownness of your skin and the crimp in your hair and the centuries in your eyes. You can bathe in love as if you were sitting comfortably in my heart. You can feel the energy of my love, pulling you through the vision of your unlimited expression. I am not asking you to love anyone other than yourself—but to love your soft edges as well as the rough—to be tender to you and to see the divine in all of your sisters. My love is exactly where you are. My love is here, right here, commanding you to ask for whatever your soul desires. My love is here, calling you to receive its bountiful blessings. My love is here, on the wings of every desire, the anticipation of every thought, the sanctity of every moment, acknowledging that your pure wishes will be granted. Your wishes born of love will be granted.

No matter how your life appears, my love is here, begging you to knock at the portal of infinite possibilities. My love is here, pulling you from the past and blessing you with the present. My love is here, dancing deliberately inside the beauty that you shine from your inseparable connection to all that God truly is.

I am here as love, painting each corner of the universe with something holy—something that you can latch onto and smile—something that you can call your own. I am here baptizing your longings in this delicious mixture that you call life, pulsating with fresh ideas on the path of your awakening. Move with my grace. Marvel in my song. Make music without fear that you will not be accepted. You are my love radiating me in every corner of the planet. Catch a glimpse of my face in your reflection. Find my mantra in your mosque. Bow to the divine in you when you recite my scripture in your temple. Praise the love in you when you find my salvation into your church. Practice my presence and stop withholding your love from others.

Stop weighing your love on a proverbial scale to protect yourself from love-thieves—those you fear will use you and squander your love and never, ever return it. There is no need to conserve this divine energy that flows through you because the one who loves with all her heart really does triumph. I look forward to a time when you will understand what John meant when he said "God is love." He said that "Whoever lives in love lives in God, and God in him" (1 John 4:16). This clear mandate is the only religion that you need. For if you guided yourselves by a religion of unconditional love, there would be no room for hatred or discord or wars or famine. If you truly loved your neighbors as yourself, there would be no room for condemnation or prejudice or mean-spiritedness about anything or anyone—especially your sisters. There would not even be a need for a Valentine just to express your love for each other.

కొ∽

FROM HER SCROLL CALLED CREATION

By the time Eve was born, humanity struggled to remember its soul. Karmic fear became jealousy, rage and distrust. Sisters and brothers created wars when there were none. Strife continued, even after conflict had long been resolved.

Grace tried to intercede when she could, but their consciousness expanded—multiplying throughout earthly kingdoms and conscious realms until Karma knew every creature beginning, every path unfolding, and every end transforming.

Grace simply watched over all, guided all, completed all, harmonized all. Karma occupied herself with the details of right and wrong—good and bad—just and unjust. Some of her children reflected her good side and some her bad—not realizing that they were all aspects of a complete whole. The entire Universe was constantly expressing itself in unforgettable colors and good vibrations and invigorating acts of compassion.
Ultimately, they were all the daughters and sons of Love. Love was always expressing through them, always blessing through them, always giving way to their greatest good. Love taught them how to dance with healing energy power and joy. Love taught them how to be peace, harmony, and enlightenment. Love taught them how to improve life, praise differences and reap success. Love taught them how to bless, restore and surpass even their own expectations.

Breathe in Me

Squeeze prayers from summer laughing,
lift praise fingers snapping,
join movements powerfully pushing,
beckon testimonies tickling,
twist joyful tears awakening,
realize prophecies telling...you are here,
you are now,
you are forever.
శం∽ర

Breathe in me. In each breath that you take, you awaken to your power. In each breath that you take, you know that you have nothing to fear. My love will flow through your entire being with the protection, peace and awareness of my presence. My love will flow through you as infinite power, an omnipotence that can conquer any difficulty.

Philippians 4:6 tells you how much I love you. You should not be anxious about anything, just give your requests to me. I will give you anything that you ask for. There is no need to worry. I will protect you from monsters, villains, assailants and other haters. I hold you close, always in my heart. Those are my fingers massaging your scalp. Those are my hands caressing your feet. That is me—healing you in any bed of affliction. In my heart, I go before you and do the work that needs to be done. I make sure that the right people appear on your path and the right circumstances give way to what is best for you.

My challenges are only so that you are prepared for any test. You are not here merely to collect diamonds but to make sure that all of your rough edges are made smooth. I prepare you to perform what you are appointed to do. No job is too difficult, no path is too treacherous, no mountain is too high for you to take. I do the work that I appoint you to do (Job 23:14).

I call your fleeting challenges the "appearances of things." These hurdles appear in the physical world but they are always girded by my good. Just remember that if I am for you, no one can be against you (Romans 8:31). Even what another intends as evil, I will transform into your good (Genesis 50:20). I will strengthen you and help you; I will uphold you with my righteous right hand (Isaiah 41:10). That is me greasing your scalp with penetrating love. That is me surpassing all of your threshold tests. See my angels slapping high fives at your victory? That is me running the last lap of your race. You were tired, so I gave you my wings.

That is me arranging for you to fall in the arms of a really good lover, a really great spouse, a lasting friend. I did that because you remembered to seek the kingdom first. I love to add all of the other details: the dozens of roses, the petals strewn, the silk sheets, the warm oils, the candle lights reminding you both that I am the true source. When you know me, the gift of your love will be so profound that it will transform everyone you meet. When you center in me, in Spirit, I will pour through you without ceasing. I will be your everlasting shield, your mighty sword, your sacred breath. Breathe in me.

FROM HER SCROLL CALLED CREATION

As soon as Eve could talk, she delivered gut-wrenching sermons about why Karma should be the final word in life and death and rebirth. She had the gift of persistency from the generations before her and harbored the holier than thou attitude that sinners were meant to be punished. When the sun rose, Eve rose with it—evangelical and unforgiving in her pursuit of lost souls who needed to be baptized in the waters of Karma's foreboding redemption. Through her creative imagination, Eve thought the story of life should be cast as good and evil, which was much more exciting—a melodramatic play about gardens and trees and death and storms and battle. She strolled through the villages of Africa with her nose held high and told the stories so often that after awhile no one really knew truth from fiction. She was a sho' nough mess. In order to teach her the true lesson of benevolence, Love decided to allow her soul to live the lives of her own stories, to star in each one of her struggles until her soul deepened enough to know that the one who loves always triumphs.

I AM Sweeter Than Chocolate

You are the beginning and end of your love story.
ॐॐ

I cannot tell you enough that my power, that eternal presence of me that can best be called love, has a lot less to do with what you get and is generated far more by what you give. When you love as me, your energy of love multiplies in the universe without end and resonates in the hearts of everyone. You can never truly experience it pouring, streaming, and flowing into your life until you give it. It is like chocolate, only sweeter. You can never receive chocolate until you first open up and let it in. The more you close your heart to love and try to be selfish and condescending and frugal and afraid, the greater you seal the door shut against all your own blessings.

Now don't get me wrong. I am not promoting candy. In fact, I am wary of your resistance, those times when your door is shut to me—you try to fill yourself up with chocolate, and soda pop, and cake, and cookies, and ice cream, and pie, and all of life's artificial sweeteners and stimulants and intoxicants. I want you to be receptive to my sweetness. I am sweeter than any source known to humanity, and I am calorie-free. You can enjoy as much of me as you wish without a trip to the doctor, the dentist or the dietician. I am your health and your wholeness, your peace and your contentment. I am the only love that you need, and I am the only love that can satisfy you.

John is correct that whoever does not love does not know God because I am love. I am reciprocal—give and take. My love is not romance but an open response to all that you give of you. My love is infinite in your life here and after. I am sweeter and more lasting than chocolates, more lasting than a relationship in the flesh. I am always blessing you, always protecting you, always answering your prayers, always giving you what you need.

My love for you is magnified by your love for each other. Are you demonstrating my good in order to take care of someone else's needs or just worried about your own? Are you doing whatever you can through the power that I AM to transform all that is violent, cruel and cold to what is loving, peaceful, forgiving? Are you ready to stop suffering? Are you compassionate to those around you? Are you feeding the poor, clothing the needy, healing the sick—or doing whatever you can to put an end to them? I will end your strife in the world when you end strife in your heart. I will only do for you what I can demonstrate through you.

Are you expressing me within you or just waiting for Valentine's Day? Are you trying to find the right person, or trying to be the right person? The question never is *what have you done for me lately* but *what can I do for you now? How can I make you laugh? How can I ease your burden? How can I lift your spirit? How can I heal your soul? How can I ease your despair and walk with you to the healing pool of your redemption? How can I remind you of the blessing that you are? How can I be sweeter to you than chocolate?* I am the beginning and end of your love story.

ॐॐ
FROM HER SCROLL CALLED EVOLUTION

I am the time before,
the has been,
the until then,
the beginning now.
When no one knows my name,
when everyone has long forgotten,
your soul will see me in the darkness, and remember.

I am the breath-filled space,
the light-filled hand,
the love-filled heart,
the joy-filled dance.
When all eyes are wearily closing,
prayers call to me, miracles climb from my
wings, and I anoint believers with the whispers of
sweet dreams.

I am the moment spared,
the twist of fate,
the nick of time,
the just missed.
When everyone is busy looking for God, as something
more extraordinary than themselves, they will miss
me, even though I am here.

ॐॐ

Dance Beyond Done
and Do Even More

Arise

Your skeletons will dance their way out of your closets—not to curse you
but to bless you
with the opportunity to change.

෯෨෯

My beloved Nelson Mandela said, "It always seems impossible until it is done." South Africa is a constant reminder of suffering in the midst of prosperity. I hear its cry for freedom, justice, and equality everywhere because everywhere someone is suffering. South Africa is one of many lessons that nothing is impossible. The children of Soweto gave their lives to lead the way. Realizing their call, they brought lasting change. Gandhi felt their spirit when he proclaimed that you must "be the change that you want to see in the world." Mandela said "In my country, first we are prisoners, then we become Presidents." Even though he was neither prisoner nor an enslaved African, Barack Hussein Obama also demonstrates this truth in my United States. Nothing is impossible.

I have destined you for universal greatness—not just as mother and co-creator but as healer and innovator and scientist and leader and motivator and transformer and molder and shaper and legislator and educator and provider and transgressor. The world is suffering because sexism, greed and exploitation has burdened and weakened those who should be cherished. It is up to you—not merely to get the job done but to dance beyond done and do even more. Stop bickering, fighting and gossiping amongst yourselves, and do the impossible task. Do the deliverance work. Do the good that you have long been awaiting. Rise up as the divine diva that you are and take responsibility for my world. Where you have held back, you must press forward. Where you have laid low, you must aim higher. Where you have said no, you must say yes. Where you have been in darkness, you must see the light. Where you have limited yourself to old norms, you must pour energy into new beginnings.

You carry the seeds of change within your soul. You have the power to plant them in the universe. You have the ability to water them. You have the ability to watch them grow, and see them illuminate the greatness in you. You struggle only because you fail to help each other, and thus fail to help yourself. Within you is the seed of peace and the greatness of my unlimited resources. You are your sister's and your brother's keeper. You are the new wine, and you cannot be contained in old wine skins. Whatever it is that you want; whatever it is that you need; whatever it is that you pray for, it is done. All you have to do is move forward with renewed energy to attain it. As Nelson Mandela said, it only seems impossible until you realize it in consciousness. You are the dance. You are the disciple. You are the deliverance. Move beyond your disbelief and do even more than you could ever imagine. Just take one step, and I will take two.

⟡

FROM HER SCROLL MARKED CREATION

*But after she had roamed the universe for millions of years—as we know
them, Grace decided that she would transcend the earth plane and
communicate through the breath of life amongst all beings.
She would simply ride the wind,
continue the journey of the breath
and manifest in the vortex of prayer.*

*Karma and Mandla decided to depart with Grace. Their departure
caused the earth to shake, volcanoes to erupt, icebergs to shudder and tsu-
namis to pour. When all was still, they existed in the flesh no longer.*

*People gathered crystals, stones, rocks, shawls, scarves, rings, earrings,
blankets imbued with their power and their scent. Then they looked
at these piles of stuff, and they wept. Some of the children, now great-
great great grandparents themselves, took something as a keepsake in
case memories soon forgot, except for those who remembered. Night quiet
anointed them with the dreams of dark, brown, black, peace, swift, silent,
space, tomorrow until there was nothing left of them in the physical realm,
but bones.*

*After Grace, Karma and Mandla had made their transition to the spirit
world, Myrtle—a small child—got up before anyone else did to go to
where their bodies had been buried and their souls had ascended in the
wind. Grace had been like Myrtle's mother because Grace kept her precious
soul and rocked her to sleep at night, always showing her that Love would
be with her.*

⟡

You Are Precious

Surrender to the victory that you are.
Call forth your extraordinary power.
Nothing can contain your strong body,
brilliant mind and loving soul.
Your midnight brown is greater than glory.
Your cinnamon coffee is sweeter than salvation.
Your deep earth red is stronger than holy.
I am so that you are.

๛

When Monique won an Oscar for Best Supporting Actress in the movie *Precious*, I was not only elated because of her accomplishment, but because the ministry that she continuously displays through her craft as an actress was shining for you to see in a phenomenal way. Whenever you see Monique, you feel the soul-stirring sincerity of her commitment to people and her vision to use art to not just entertain, but to promote change in your consciousness. Not only do you laugh with her, but you cry with her; you grow strong with her; and most importantly, you become wiser because of her.

She reminds you to love yourself. She teaches you that you don't have to look like emaciated models or anything other than who you are to be loving and liberated and loved. She teaches you that you can be dignified and strong and determined, as well as gracious and glorious and fine. She teaches you that you need to face your problems head on so that you can begin to do the healing work that all communities need. She teaches us that you can be victorious simply by doing what is right. *What better lesson is there than that?*

Monique's acceptance speech was gracious and poignant. Among other words of recognition, she thanked the Academy for doing what was "right." She said that it wasn't about the politics, it was about the performance. She also thanked her husband for convincing her to forego doing what was popular in order "to do what's right."

Sapphire's book *Push* is the story that the movie *Precious* is based on. It's the story of an African American girl growing up in the most abusive home imaginable. The most horrific thing about the story is that it's real. This is part of the truth that you must face, of the abuse that you are suffering every day. Every moment, youth of all ages are being abused by their parents and other adults and have no one to help them but me. I show up through your obedience, when you listen. I have asked you repeatedly to help your sisters and your daughters and your nieces and your friends. I have begged you to stop feeling sorry for yourself and help them *PUSH*. *Push* past the obstacles; *push* past the pain; *push* out of the hell-hole that they live in and find a better place in Spirit. If you haven't seen *Precious* or read the book *PUSH,* now is the time to do it. Most importantly, now is the time to open your own consciousness to do what is right. And if you think you can't, well...*Push.*

If you push forward, I will push you. Listen to my Spirit when I tell you to push, when I tell you to lift, when I tell you to move. Listen to my Spirit when I tell you to let go, when I tell you to release, when I tell you to leave. Listen to my Spirit when I tell you to trust, when I tell you to leave, when I tell you throw away anything that is not consistent with my greatest good. You are better than the greatest thing that anyone in the flesh can give you. You are better than you could ever imagine. You are better than the ground upon which you walk and the eyes through which you see. Never, ever stop trusting in me. As Jesus said in Matthew 5:29-30, "If your right eye causes you to sin, gouge it out and throw it away. It is better for you to lose one part of your body than for your whole body to be thrown into hell. And if your right hand causes you to sin, cut it off and throw it away. It is better for you to lose one part of your body than for your whole body to go into hell." I am the almighty power and I am in you. I am your constant source of supply, unlimited in good. Stop second-guessing your divine nature. My loved ones should never suffer because you don't have the courage to free them from their pain.

Reach beyond the boundaries of the norm and the conventional to be the woman that I anointed you to be. Know that even in your darkest hour, you can *push,* knowing that you are my precious child. Say *"Come Holy Spirit come, fill this space within me that has not yet realized you are here. Come Holy Spirit, take me across the great divide of everything that keeps me from being all that I can be—and show me your power; make your presence known. Come Holy Spirit, take me over the Jordan that only good can cross and breathe through me my destiny, the triumph of my soul, the dynamic being that I AM. Come Holy Spirit, take me through waters on dry land, and use me to serve you with faith. Come Holy Spirit, come and shine your light through me."*

FROM HER SCROLL MARKED CREATION

In that moment, Myrtle felt something that she had never felt before, a longing to be with Grace: a longing to smell her scent of aloe and thyme, a longing to see the rhythm of her movement, always patient, deliberate, compassionate. In her longing, she sat weeping until her soul began to sleep, where she saw her Grace.

Grace had shown her that she would return. Grace had shown her that she would never leave her. Grace had shown her that she would be there— beneath the myrtle tree. The myrtle whose trunk was as brown as Grace, if not browner, the color of sweet mother earth, the color of beginnings when all colors came and blended with themselves, the deep color of possibility.

Under the myrtle tree, Grace felt the potential and the pure possibility of her new niece, even before she was born. Myrtle enjoyed the rivers coursing through the earth's veins, and at the fat fingers of her soon-to-be brothers and sisters, playing in the thick mud. She saw the beautiful branches of the trees that lined the entrance to Grace's garden. It was as if the child heard what the trees were called, and in that instant was also named Myrtle. All of her elders felt her Spirit.

Come Home to Spirit

Lift prayers from souls laughing,
hear wisdom's fingers snapping,
join movements powerfully giving,
leave love always reaping,
realize prophetic voices calling,
know deep rhythms singing...
you are here,
you are here.

～☙

My indigenous people know that where you are born is connected with your soul forever. No matter how many miles you move away, you will find yourself longing to return.

You see that with Jesus in the Bible. Nazareth, his home, was in Galilee, and if you read the scriptures carefully, you will see Jesus returned there again and again for spiritual nourishment. When Jesus returns to Galilee something phenomenal always happens because he is not just returning home in the physical, he is returning home in consciousness. He returns to an increased receptivity to my power moving in him.

Jesus taught that the Prodigal Son returned home after he had squandered his wealth. But his Father welcomed him with open arms. This wasteful son had gone to the "far country" where he squandered his money with "riotous living." In a weak economy, he ended up with a job that required him to feed the swine—and he himself fed off the husks that the swine ate. But one day, he finally came to his senses and said to himself: "I will arise and go to my Father."

I am always saying come home to me, but some of y'all keep running in the opposite direction. Understand that when the Prodigal Son returned home, his Father immediately said "Bring forth quickly the best robe and put it on him, and put a ring on his finger, and shoes on his feet. And bring the fatted calf and kill it and let us eat and make merry, for this my son was dead and is alive again. He was lost and now is found." This is my way of trying to teach you that if you come home, if you find your way back to Spirit, all that you believe you lost will be restored. If you come home, you will taste the unlimited power of the universe and realize the unlimited good of my kingdom. If you come home, I will not just feed you, I will give you a feast. I will bring out the fatted calf of unlimited substance, life in its fullest, all of the things that you have been praying for.

All you have to do is leave the far country and come home. Leave the far country of limited thinking; leave the far country of fear; leave the far country where you were too busy—didn't have the time—completely forgot to center in Spirit. Don't worry about where you will sleep. I keep telling you that there are many rooms in my mansion, I will go there to prepare a place for you. I am your shepherd, you shall never want. I will shower you with infinite gifts. Don't worry about your feet, if you come home to me, I will anoint your feet with the strength to stand under all things; and in your understanding, you will have the wisdom that you need. Don't worry about the time that you missed or the mistakes that you made, I will restore your divine inheritance. You are heir to my throne. You will never want again. All that I have is yours. Goodness and mercy will be with you all days of your life.

I have taught you to pray: each time you pray, you will come home to me. I have taught you to meditate: each time you close your eyes and focus on my breath, you will come home to me. I have taught you to ask: each time you allow my blessings to fill your life by opening your heart to receive, you will come home to me.

Beloved, this is the season to come home. Leave the far country of despair and be guided by the realization that my love is unconditional and complete. I never judge you, never vex you, never condemn you, I just simply await your return.

FROM HER SCROLL MARKED CREATION

*Like Grace, Myrtle knew that she was Spirit expressed as Flesh. Her eyes
sparkled deep cinnamon brown—like the magical twists of tiny roots and
vines growing from her head. She moved her first steps knowing, believing, surrendering, uplifting, recognizing. In each step, she remembered all
there was to know about the world she was in because she was far less a
child than she was a God. Like Grace, wherever Myrtle wanted to be, she
was; whatever Myrtle wanted to grow, she grew; whenever Myrtle wanted
to create, she created—generations of civilizations, centuries of poems,
universes of angels that she could summon through the power that she
was. Like Grace, Myrtle knew that she was the Alpha and the Omega, the
first and the last, the beginning and the end. She knew that she was born
for a purpose, and it was her intention to do
what Love had called her to do..... .*

*Her sister Essie quietly emerged with the delicious grain bread that Myrtle
loved, olives warmed by the sun, figs, and honey. She brought warm
quilts, and a jug of water from the stream. And there, the two of them sat
until Jessie, Lena and Benjamin, the eldest, came and made them a fire.
They watched it in a way that they knew the memory of it
would last in their souls forever.*

Taste the Bread of Life

Taste the bread of life.
Drink living water.
Push away from the table of your enemies.
Get up from your mat of affliction.
Stir the waters of Spirit.
And then fly, fly on the wings of faith.

कॐ◌ऊ

There is so much fear around you today that you have started worshipping it like an idol, which is no different than melting a golden calf. Joshua said *choose* this day whom you will serve. Choose whether you want to worship what is distributed, manufactured, traded, bought, sold, mortgaged, melted down by man, or whether you want to worship God, Spirit, Divine Source, Infinite Wisdom—or whatever you call the flow of good always expressing itself. Here's a clue: there is never a recession in Spirit. You forget that you are believers and yet you ignore the 6th Chapter of Matthew, when Jesus told you not to worry. He said to seek first the kingdom of God, and all the material things that you need or desire will be given to you as well.

You see, in Exodus 35:13, I told Moses to tell the Israelites to make a table, and to set it with plates and dishes of pure gold, and to put on it the bread of presence. This table of bread represents universal substance, there for you to partake at all times. This means that all of the substance of the universe is always present. You do not have to get more substance; all the substance of the Universe is right where you are.

You are created of substance, formed of substance, supported by substance. The stuff that happens around you and to you doesn't matter. The only thing that matters is what happens within you.

It does not matter what material things you get; what matters is whether you are expressing your divine nature. Manna, the bread of life, is so abundant that no one ever need have less in order for you to have more. You do not need to compete for the bread of life.

In Luke 6:38, Jesus said give and it will be given to you. Give to the people around you: give compassion, give love, give food, give clothing, give financial resources, give kindness, give hugs, give listening. Give the gifts that you have, and you immediately open the wellspring of blessings from the Universe from me to you. My sources are infinite, which means that your good comes from so many channels, you cannot begin to imagine where it will come from. Often it's the person least expected. Many times, your good comes from the person that you find it hardest to forgive. But when you are truly connected to my inexhaustible supply, your order will always be filled. Manna will appear as the blessings, the guidance, the opportunity, the skills, the abilities, the ideas, the success that you need whenever you need it.

I am the bread of life. You who come to me will never go hungry. You who believe in me will never thirst. If anyone eats of my bread, she will live forever. My bread is the substance that continues to feed you, even when you think you are broke. It's that *way out of no way*; it's that neighbor who shows up with a bag of food; it's that fifty dollar bill that suddenly falls out of a pocket; it's that money that you find on the street. My bread is the unseen goodness that you are always surrounded by—just waiting for you tap it. In the unseen, you are always receiving a blessing. You feel the magnitude of this blessing when you are centered in me. Otherwise, you will miss the most phenomenal bread you have ever tasted.

ॐॐ

ॐ⌖

FROM HER SCROLL MARKED CREATION

*Just as they awakened, Grace appeared. She was like a light. She was so
radiant that she shined with her entire being. Stars shined in her eyes; her
body glistened like chocolate in the moist air; her hair flowed in the wind
as she left movements forever etched in time for those who came after to
remember. She said nothing, but her presence celebrated all that was and
ever would be.... If you could have seen their eyes in the instant that they
felt Truth fill their hearts, you would know that they got what we call the
Holy Ghost. In that instant, Myrtle felt her body lift off the ground, and
she began to weep. Her brother and her sister hugged her, grateful that
they too could be a witness.*

*Grace embraced her niece, and when she did,
Myrtle could feel all the other souls that had moved on. Myrtle felt prayers
of worlds unveiled, laughter of living water, cups running over, psalms of
peace unspoken. Grace almost seemed to glide. She moved triumphantly
with the Spirit. And as she did the holy dance of the ages, she seemed to
slowly fade
with the wind that carried her.*

*As Grace disappeared in the wind, Myrtle could see children to come on
the mountains, in the valleys and at the sea beyond—feeling the wind
through their hair and at their backs. Perhaps some would learn that the
wind was Grace, breathing through them Truth that they would remember
through the passage of time—
to honor Love—and to know that by so doing so,
they honored themselves.*

ॐ⌖

Have No Fear

Spirit move me past my limiting thoughts
so that I move forward with a new vision,
so that I can release my fears,
so I can dance like a hip hop tune
to the beat of a power-infused rhythm.

୨୦

Dear Daughter, do not forget that—despite the appearances of the stock market, the bail-out plan, the folding institutions, the loss of jobs and homes, and the fear that attempts its way into your mind—you are still heirs to my throne. You always remain in my kingdom. You continue to dwell in the secret place of the most high and abide under my shadow. This means that you must stay tuned into my Spirit, in every word that you speak, in every thought that you think, in every breath that you breathe. I am your refuge and your fortress. I am all you need. Yes, I will deliver you from the snare of the fowler and from the noisome pestilence. I will cover you with my feathers and under my wings you must trust. I am your shield and buckler. I know what you have need of before you even ask. So no matter what the circumstances, fear not.

Do not be bothered by the terror by night, nor for the arrow that flieth by day, nor for the pestilence that walketh in darkness, nor for the destruction that wastes at noonday. My abundance always pours, streams, flows through you—and is available to you as long as you are willing to receive it. A thousand shall fall at your side and ten thousand at your right hand, but it will not impact you when you allow me to be the source that you center in. Shake the dust off your shoes and keep moving on my path. My angels will take charge over you and keep you safe in all my ways.

Riding out the turmoil around you is sort of like riding the subways in New York. You board the subway with faith, having no idea where the train may take you but still trust that somehow you will get to your destination. Subway trains break down, stop completely, re-route to different lines, and sometimes even take you non-stop to destinations that you never anticipated. But you can ride through any storm if you pray as, in and through me.

Prayer is when you acknowledge that I am. Pray boldly. Pray courageously. Pray persistently. Pray in your homes, lodges, halls, churches, synagogues, mosques, temples. Don't limit your prayers to bent knees, bowed heads or church pews. Pray in the car, the street, the bus, the subway. Pray for the conductor and engineer. Pray for every person in the subway car. Pray for people on the platforms. Pray for the people on the street. Pray for the people in your community, city, country, world. Pray like Moses. Pray like Job. Pray like Paul. Pray like Jesus in his secret place. Don't only ask that those who have lost their homes, jobs, savings, investments, and hope be restored but that your financial institutions, government and leaders be strengthened, sustained and enlightened.

Ask that this unraveling somehow serve as the healing that you need to uplift those who have always been impoverished, sick and distraught, those who have never had stock plans, pension funds, bank accounts, job security or home equity. I promise you only one thing: your prayers will be answered. I am in charge. I have no reserve, no budget, no limit. No one and nothing can break the back of my currency. No institution, no market, no bank, no man can destroy, derail, or even delay what is moving forward from my station. Keep this Truth first and foremost in your mind—that when you pray you become part of the energy that will bring about change. Nothing and no one can keep your good from you. If you pray, you will see everyone that you've prayed for—blessed in ways that you could never imagine.

෨෧

༰~ঙ

FROM HER SCROLL MARKED CREATION

Love didn't need words. Words have their power but also their limits.
Words rode the power of intention through the wind and from that energy
all thoughts emerged and took the shape of the heart, mind and soul that
intended them. Power came before the words. Divine vibrations erupted
and universal energy clothed it with sound. Sound touched the recipient
and word was born in and of itself.

Myrtle watched words get stuck in the earth that contained them, bur-
ied in the winters that over time forgot how they began. She saw words
migrate from the warm bosoms of mothers, nurse from the inexhaustible
milk of delivery, and stop remembering. Words hardened like bones and
stopped listening to themselves.

Words were always besides themselves with enthusiasm, dropping from
mouths everywhere, pulling themselves from hearts with intent, falling
from mouths with amazement. Words tied themselves into scrolls, re-wrote
themselves, redacted others and followed history across the walls of temples
now unknown to humanity. But after so many words had been created,
after so many years had passed, words rotted in the teeth of liars and froze
in the hearts of thieves—until no one remembered, and no one dared to
ask. How could there be a Father—without a Mother?

Create Outside the Box of Conventionality

こん

FROM HER SCROLL MARKED CREATION

New souls gathered at Myrtle's feet as words rose from her spirit, then took to the wind. Only the wind was everywhere present in the cracks and crevices of the universe as her children built new nations—to learn, to see, to enhance, to propel, to spin, to move, to marvel.

"Stop your fighting and your bickering over mere opinions," she would say. "Life presents endless opportunities to be different. Love was your creator. And in the unconditional spirit of love, you must open your heart and stay in tune to your divine purpose. Whatever you love to do will be your calling, which will raise in you the genius of your own sacred expression of good. A time will come when there will be poets among you, those who understand the power of the word, who will speak this Truth, saying 'You are the ones that you have been waiting for.'
There will be prophets among you, who will teach this Truth, warning 'You are the love that you seek.' There will be painters would recreate this Truth, showing 'You can only love yourself by always being honest.' There will even be potters who will carry this Truth, remembering 'You are part and parcel of God's love that is always present in and as us.' There will always be Shamans among you, who will heal through this Truth, always prescribing Love: 'if you do not feel good about who you are, no one else can.'"

こん

Step Outside Your Box into Imagination

Brown girls hold the light of eternity within—to remember that there is nothing that they cannot do, nothing that they cannot be, nothing that they cannot summon in who they are—not something less but something more; not someone weaker but someone stronger; not somewhere distant—but but always right in the arms of love.

ॐ◦ॐ

In Deuteronomy 34: 1-4, it says: "Then Moses climbed Mount Nebo from the plains of Moab to the top of Pisgah, across from Jericho. There the Lord showed him the whole land—from Gilead to Dan...." Then I said to him, "This is the land I promised on oath to Abraham, Isaac and Jacob when I said 'I will give it to your descendants.' I have let you see it with your eyes, but you will never cross over into it." Moses was allowed to see but not cross over into the Promised Land. Metaphysically, Moses is not a person; Moses is a consciousness. Moses is that part of you that seeks the higher things of the Spirit but has not yet reached a full acceptance of the *creative power* within.

Your creative power has several dimensions. Your creative abilities give you the power to see, envision, imagine—to be open and receptive to the ideas that will help you manifest the good that you were called to produce. Moses could *see* God because he had achieved that state of consciousness where he could envision Absolute Good. He was a High Priest in Egypt of the highest degree. He could ascend to the highest realm in meditation and fasting and do most of what I called him to do, but he was not yet in that state of consciousness where he could believe his true worth.

An important aspect of your creative power lies in your belief—your ability to say yes to the ideas that you desire to express through your life. This creative consciousness exists to assist you in the manifestation of your good, which is good for all humanity. Whatever you are called to create has a domino effect of creativity for all of those around you. But you cannot hold back; you cannot be afraid; you cannot be a nay-sayer.

To a large extent, Moses was a nay-sayer. He didn't believe what I told him to do. I told him to go talk to the people, and he said—me?! I can't talk; I'm not a good speaker. Then I said well I will send your brother Aaron to speak for you. I told Moses to use my rod for a demonstration of his power, and Moses said huh? What's that gonna to do? And I said just do what I said, and he was astonished that it turned into a snake. When Moses asked "who should I tell them sent me?" I said "tell them I AM that I AM." But he still didn't get it. He still didn't really believe the Absolute Good expressing through him.

In the Book of Numbers, when I instructed Moses to speak to the rock to bring forth water—Moses didn't believe what I said. Instead, he struck the rock with his rod twice—saying that he would bring forth water. A consciousness that does not believe cannot co-create with me to move to the next level—what some call "the Promised Land." Your power to create pushes you beyond the edge of what you as a human can do to the greatness of what I can do through you. I am the co-creative force of every breath that you breathe and every bit of energy that you expel. When you forget that you are divine ideas; when you just look at what you can do in the flesh; when you stop tapping into and turning on my infinite power, you cannot reach the Promised Land. The journey is not about you, it is about my creative power expressing as you.

Yet, when you trust fully and completely in me without all of your second-guessing, you stop limiting what you can do in the flesh and start creating through the energy that has summoned you to this existence. You become the "Joshua" in consciousness—the I AM that I AM, the full anointing of Spirit. Only then will you cross over into the Promised Land. Wings will take shape from your soul and deliver you beyond your imaginings—across the threshold of your fears. Magic and miracles and divine openings in the universal fabric of Spirit will manifest. You will begin to do God's Work. You will envision, imagine, and create by saying YES—with all of your hearts, minds, and souls—YES!

Yes, you should say: "I forgive myself for what I didn't do before—for all of the days that I didn't step up to the plate, for those times when I allowed my human-ness to refrain from giving 1000% percent, for being undisciplined, for not listening, for being reluctant to see beyond what human eyes can see. I forgive myself, and I tap the creative power of the universe. I step over the edge—beyond the boundaries that have limited me for so long and I surrender."

Surrender with the Spirit of Rosa Parks. How many times had she taken that bus and walked to the back, when she was tired, when she needed a seat, when she was afraid to listen to the creative power within? Surrender with the Spirit of Harriet Tubman. How many times had she been beaten? How many times had she been treated like an animal? How many times had she watched her family suffer until she tapped the creative power within? Surrender with the Spirit of Fannie Lou Hammer. How many times had she wanted to cast her vote? How many times had she suffered from not ever experiencing equal rights and justice—before she stood up and said "I'm sick and tired or being sick and tired"?

Surrender to the realization that you can't do my work on your own. Say: Yes, I have to step outside of the shackles that enslave me. I don't know how I'm going to get 'cross the Jordan. I don't have a boat and I don't have money to buy a boat. I see the road ahead of me, and I don't know where it leads, but I welcome the creative energy of Spirit to bear witness to a world that empowers me.

Say: Yes, I will go all the way to the edge. I will let go of what I know and allow myself to be led by Spirit's creative energy. I won't worry about changing who I am. I will accept everything about me that I know and allow myself to meet the parts of me that I don't know. I will trust that whatever I need to create from, I already have in the creative power that God expresses as me."

Saying YES to me removes the shackles of your past, opens up the barriers of your present, and erases the chains of despair from your future. Allow the unexpected, the untested, the untamed, and the unknown to guide you on whichever path I give you and take it to the end. You will not fall off. You are strong enough to make a difference, pretty enough, smart enough, important enough, creative enough.

Exercise your divine power of creativity here and now to cut off your thoughts of limitation and lack and fear and doubt, and start saying yes to the divine ideas that you have already received. "Yes, I can open my new business. Yes, I can finish my new book. Yes, I can plant that garden of greatness. Yes, I can triumph through the gifts and talents that Spirit has given me. Even if things appear to have chaos and struggle and strife, I know that Spirit never stops giving me the creative power to bring out of that chaos wonderful new gifts."

Messiness is the soil of your creation. Just letting go and allowing yourself to be will honor the intuitive voice in you that is always speaking, always leading, always showing you how to stir up the ingredients that you need, how to mix the right formula, how to trust that everything is coming together for your greatest good.

Infinite paths lead to the manifestation of your dreams, but only I can bring you to the other side. You will cross the Jordan of your doubt, or your pain, or your worry, or your fear when you evolve through it. When you use your challenges as a bridge to surrender to me, when you turn not to the left—nor to the right but to the kingdom within, when you move beyond "I can't" to "I can", you will find that you have already touched the shores of the Promised Land.

FROM HER SCROLL MARKED CREATION

"Just remember," my children, Myrtle taught.
"If you remember where you came from, whose image and likeness you were
made in, you will have the answer to every prayer."
She said, "Some of you will call yourselves Jews and you will teach: 'What
is hateful to you, do not do to your fellow man. That is the entire law; all
the rest is commentary.' Some of you will call yourselves Brahmans, and
you will say: 'This is the sum of duty: Do naught unto others which would
cause you pain if done to you.' Some of you will call yourselves Buddhists,
and you will write: 'Hurt not others in ways that you yourself would find
hurtful.' Some of you will call yourselves Taoists, and you will know: 'Re-
gard your neighbor's gain as your own gain and your neighbor's loss as
your own loss.' Some of you will call yourselves Christians, and you will
immortalize these words: 'So in everything, do to others what you would
have them do to you, for this sums up the Law and the Prophets.' Some of
you will not choose religion or God but you will know deep in your soul
these laws and you will be able to make a decision for love is always in
our soul—for we are not separate from it. Embracing these principles of
Truth is simply one way of recognizing who we are. Those who do will be
the most powerful among people; they will manifest their greatest dreams
as much as they embrace their divine connection with Love."

Step Outside Your Box
and into Blessings

Brown girls awaken to the love that is always lifting you, always rais-
ing you, always feeding you, always baptizing you, always dancing you,
always singing you, always anointing you, always restoring you, always
healing you, always chanting you, always inviting you from the boxes
outside of you to the eternal power that you are.

Have you ever felt imagination move through you with mo-
mentum so powerful that you knew its energy was not just you—but
a gift from Spirit? I am always seeking to express myself through
your gifts and talents. I am flowing through your "creative process"
to invent, to uplift, to grow, to seize, to fashion, to give birth to
something beautiful. When you let go and allow me to use you, you
will realize that there really is nothing that you cannot do in alignment with your divine purpose. You are called to be more than a
consumer, more than a service provider, more than an employee,
more than an assistant. You are called to create work for others,
to demonstrate your leadership, to be a co-partner with all that I
am. All you have to do is step outside of the box where you have
contained yourself, and accept your blessings.

What seeds have you planted in your mind that are waiting to
see the light of day? What dreams have I given you? Take them out.
Dust them off. Give them your time. Allow them to blossom. Let
them take shape. Trust yourself. As Emerson said, "to thine own
self be true." When I gave you the breath of life, I gave you gifts
that you have yet to open. The only way to experience their reward
is to step outside the box of tradition, the box of fear, the box of

caring what others think—and there you will see your blessings take shape.

FROM HER SCROLL MARKED CREATION

"I honor the Divine that birthed the unique being that I call me. I honor the Universal Ethers that formed every hair, every molecule, every fiber, every divine vibration of the I AM that I AM. I honor the Cosmic Womb that delivered the light that shines as me. I honor the Spirit that carried me into this fantastic reality that I call life. I honor the sheer passion of perfect harmony that manifested me into the endless bounty of this time space continuum that we call earth. I honor the Souls who came before me and through whose legacy I began, not simply because I am, but because without them, I would never be. I honor the Love that gave me a destiny in the irresistible vortex of my desires. I honor the Ancestors—expressing through me the love of enlightened purpose and endless possibility."

Step Outside Your Box and into Belief

*You are co-creators of life.
You carry new worlds in your hearts.
You carry new light in your souls.*

えへ

My beloved Jesus said all things are possible to whoever believes (Mark 9:23), which raises the question: *what are you believing?* Do you believe that you are not just average, or mediocre, or marginal? Do you believe that you are not too old, too busy, or too tired? Do you believe that you are not too poor, or too broke, or too needy? Do you believe that you can put aside childish things and pick up the mantle that you were born to carry—not the mantle of the weak but of the enduring spirit. Are you ready to accept my challenge to believe in your God-given right to be victorious? Do you believe in you?

If you believe in you, stop allowing the distractions of temporary pleasures—like alcohol, drugs, food, sex, soap operas, reality shows, and the other mindless games or self-perpetuated dramas that keep you from doing the work. If you believe in you, stop ignoring your energy-infused faith and instead feel its power, know its might, witness its Truth, step outside of your disbelief, and be transformed. If you believe in you, spend the time that it takes to center in your own power, so that you will see the gifts and talents that you have. If you believe in you, strengthen your belief in the power of Spirit and quicken the steps that you need to move forward with your dreams. The world anxiously awaits new leadership, new vision, new heroes, new books, new legends, new cures, new designs, new hope, new success. Now is the time to roll up your sleeves, bite the bullet, press forward, tear down if necessary—but most importantly to rebuild, to plant, to plow, to lift, to create, to nurture, to weed, to compose, to shine, to flow, to grow, to do all of the good that you desire. But you cannot accomplish your goals or step into your greatness from the confines of a box.

ॐ ॐ

FROM HER SCROLL MARKED VICTORY

If you are waiting by the healing pool
for someone to lift you in;
if you are reaching to touch the garment of wholeness;
if you are weary in the race and cannot go any further;
if you are down in the valley and need some lifting up,
then all you have to do is call my name.

I am greater than you could ever imagine.
I am the healing balm, the burning bush,
the living water.
I can walk through the fire, cut to the chase,
rise to the occasion.
I never lose, never miss, never falter.
I am closer to you than hands and feet,
closer to you than the air that you breathe
and the space that you take up.
Victory is my name, and you—
made in the image and likeness of God—
are all that I am.

ॐ ॐ

Step Outside Your Box
and into Freedom

Move forward on this journey—like never before.
Enjoy the blessing of realizing
that you control your life, that everything is coming together
for your greatest good,
that there is nothing that you can't do,
that Spirit is pulling you outside of the box of limitation
and lifting you in a new dimension of change,
that the sun is radiating from your soul,
and that your sisters are here,
leading the way.

૭ન૭

One of the most difficult things to do Beloved is to move forward freely. Because of your ego's desire to protect itself, revenge is a part of our psyche. You want to get back at anyone who you believe wronged you. You are motivated by revenge. If you were truly honest with yourself, you might even say that you like it. But despite the sweet sensation of revenge, you cannot accomplish your goals unless you forgive. You don't harm others, you harm yourself when you don't forgive. Someone once described anger directed towards someone else as swallowing a bottle of poison, and waiting for the other person to die. When you condemn someone, you don't punish them; you punish yourself.

When you don't forgive everything and everyone—including yourself, you put up a barrier in your consciousness that cuts off the flow of your connection to the infinite abundance of my good. It's my good pleasure to give you the kingdom, but you block the flow of good with spite and resentment. Jesus taught that you should not just forgive seventy times, but seventy-seven times. In other words, you have to live in a state of forgiveness. Sometimes you become so attached to your anger that you can't imagine life without it. But you cannot transcend your box unless you dig deep down inside and release anyone and anything that you might be holding onto. When you release animosity, you feel the freedom of a powerful liberation. Forgiveness is the catalyst of rebirth. Lack of forgiveness is the main obstacle between you and the freedom to ride into a brand new existence. So take this step now. Look at your life and everything that you believe has gone wrong and forgive. Release. Let go.

જ‍ે‍ઝ

FROM HER SCROLL CALLED VICTORY

"If you are looking for God, if you are looking for freedom, if you are looking for prosperity—all you have to do is look within. And there you will find me.

I am the ground upon which you stand, more than the economy, richer than a stimulus, better than a job.

I am the divine surplus—always giving, always forming, always molding, always shaping, always rewarding, always liberating.

If you have forgotten me, re-discover who you are, taste the wisdom of your highest self, push past your self-imposed limitations, leave the prison of your own mind, and imagine God as simple as a plain brown girl."

જ‍ે‍ઝ

Step Outside Your Box
and into Desire

*Brown girls uplift each other with
magic on new dreams, wisdom in new hopes,
belief in new desires.*

ॐॐ

Asking to receive is the most fundamental power you were born with, and also the power least used. When you want to give shape to what you desire in your life, you have to ask. But asking is without power if you don't believe. You have to believe that you are powerful enough to receive. This means that you can't sit around complaining, fretting, worrying, and doubting. When you ask, you have to ask without even the slightest, the smallest, the tiniest bit of doubt. You have to ask with confidence, courage and boldness. You can't worry about what the neighbors might say; you have to step outside of your comfort zone and ask for what you really want. But be careful what you ask for because I will give it to you so fast, it will knock you off your feet.

Don't ask for anything belonging to someone else. Ask for what you want but say if not this—something better. I will give you what you want means that if you ask for anything according to my will, I will give it to you. I know what you have need of before you even ask (Matthew 6:6-8). Did you ever think of the consequences of that? The stuff that you want is just waiting for you to ask for it. The blessings that you desire are just sitting there waiting for your request. Before you even open your mouth to ask, I have already gone before you to not just line up what you need but everything you could ever hope for. Your deepest desire is there—just outside your box, waiting to be fulfilled.

When you ask and believe, be confident enough to give thanks. Every single quality that you attribute to me—all of the power, all of the compassion, all of the patience—you have in yourself. By being grateful, you create an energy that is open and receptive to all of the good that I want to bless you with. Giving thanks is not a quid pro quo. It doesn't make any difference to me whether you give thanks or not. But it makes a difference to your consciousness, to your oneness with the divine stream of my blessings. When you ask and are grateful, you are able to speed up the process of getting what you want.

෨෩

FROM HER SCROLL CALLED VICTORY

"Move away from pointless diversions and mindless meanderings—and find purpose in the soil of your own magic. The truth is that I am mother of you all—and there is nothing that I would not do for you if you asked. I gave to you from my Soul through Love—as my Son. He is my expression. He came from the womb of this plain brown girl. Oh Beloved, no man could accomplish what I did through my obedience to the Eternal Oneness that you know as God."

෨෩

Step Outside Your Box
into Order

Brown girls gather in the arms of love to awaken to the freedom of endless possibilities, to embrace divine opportunities, to dream new dreams, to give way to quiet healings, to heed prophetic callings.

Brown girls hold hands and hearts in the name of truth, the truth that is their mother and father God—
so what does that make them?

ॐॐ

When you leave the confines of your limitations because of your belief in Spirit, you dedicate yourself to experience a new energy of enthusiasm, a new excitement and a new order. You stop feeling like the bottom is going to fall out. Your anxiety attacks disappear. The appearances around you are no longer troubling. You sense that I am in every step that you take. It is true—when you follow me, I will work out every single detail for your greatest good. I will penetrate every aspect of your being, your purpose and your vision with a new power of boldness, courage and creativity. I make sure the right people, the right resources and the right outcomes manifest.

Jesus said "Come, leave your nets, and follow me." Get out of that limited consciousness that you have, and come follow me. Come follow me, and be courageous enough to end your story of pity, your story of refuge, your story of defeat. Put down your old hang-ups and take up the mantle of a powerful new order. I will bless you with a new prophetic vision that will give you the faith to envision and exalt the things that you have never dreamed possible. I will insure that there is no battle that you cannot win, no mountain that you cannot climb, no obstacle that you cannot overcome, and no desire that you cannot manifest. Everything you do, every project that you touch will be in perfect, divine order. There is mayhem when you don't realize your potential but order when you step outside of your box and into divine power.

ॐ

FROM HER SCROLL CALLED VICTORY

"My Son was born in the vortex of my own creation of infinite wishes, spontaneous creativity, unparalleled possibilities, unmitigated joy; and he became the entry through which those who forgot they were gods could come in. He was not born of lust, he was born of salvation. He is the Hero's hero on a journey that was victorious from the start. What he tried to teach you is to know that the battle is not yours, it is Love's. That doesn't mean that the ultimate victor is someone greater than you. Love is the greatness that you are, the I AM that I AM, the AUM never ceasing, the part of you that is constantly and prophetically in the vortex of your own creation—if you would just invite yourself in. He taught that staying where you are is not an option, staying outside the greatness that you are is not an option, languishing on the edges of dreams and never manifesting them is not an option, being afraid to climb the rough side of the mountain is not an option, failing to test your wings and catapult into a whole new existence is not an option,
being less than who you are is not an option."

ॐ

Step Outside Your Box
and into Time

We are the before and the hereafter.
We go from this womb of our love to the world
—not only as children of God but as gods.
We go from this womb of our love to the world
—not only as sisters of spirit but as Spirit itself.
We go from this womb of our love to the world
—not only as energy of life
but as co-creators endlessly creating.
We go from this womb of our love to the world
—in Spirit's time, and we deliver.

&~&

You may be asking yourself where you will find the time to do all the things that you need to do. But I will send time to find you. Time will wake you up at the oddest hour. Time will offer you the unexpected twist, the uninvited obstacle, the unresolved dilemma—pushing you out of the routine into the vortex of endless possibility. Time will remind you that every moment is an invitation to change. Your days are not as random as they seem. Each day is endowed with the possibility of unlimited potential. Each second is an opportunity to express the love that I breathe as you. Each breath carries in it the anticipation of answered prayer.

Have you ever heard somebody say that everything comes together in God's time? That means that outside your box is nothing but the present moment—and it is all good. You don't have to worry because I will carry you through your sacred journey—on time. When you meet me by being courageous enough to step outside of your box of confinement, I will make sure that minutes will not matter, and restore the days of the locusts. I will make sure that every move that you make is as harmonious with time as a symphony, or a jazz beat, or rap tune at the top of the charts. You will be able to dance with hours of good overflowing. You will be able to sing a new song of days triumphing over struggle. You will be able to build victories with patience.

You will be able to sit with me at the window of life—full of new seasons. You won't worry about the yesterdays; and you won't lose sleep over the tomorrows. My time is now—the unannounced sweet tears of joy. My time releases the fear of the unknown. My time heals with quick deliverance. My time knows that you don't have time to wait, or linger, or procrastinate. My time will erase the impenetrable door of doubt, and open wide vistas of opportunity. My time will uncover the depth of eternal wisdom and send its ready knowledge straight to you in lightening speed. You will know with amazing accuracy exactly what you need to know, and when you need to know it. My time will baptize in the waters of my grace—in case you forget, I will remember.

My time will erase your doubt and teach you in an instant that I am bigger than time and wiser than appearances. I am at the finish line before you even begin the race. I am the A+ before you finish the paper. I am the trophy before you ever see it in your hands. I easily muster the time you need—to manifest the best idea, the desired partner, the well-paid job, the necessary funds, the awaited call, the completed book, the healing touch, the extraordinary miracle—all in the mere space of a moment.

You will be able to step outside of time and not only do the work that you must but also find the rest that you need. You can find rest in my consciousness, in the heart of amazing possibilities, in the soul of everlasting truth.

When you are able to get the rest that you need to center in me, you will be able to hear me again, speaking through countless voices, saying "You are not merely human, you are gods—leaping, streaming, flowing endlessly out of a universe that knows nothing but the greatest good for you. You are vibrating in the stream of dynamic energy and powerful prayers—loving and lifting without limitation. You are dancing on the brink of a breakthrough that will not settle for less. You are everything beyond the point at which you stop asking and start knowing that all that you desire is already in the divine vortex of God's making." And perhaps when you listen, you will hear: there is all the time that you need right here in me. In my time, you will have a clearer vision, a steadier walk, a more definite purpose—and no matter what, you will succeed.

ॐ⊷

FROM HER SCROLL CALLED VICTORY

*"You have in your scriptures," my Son said, "you are gods." He said "seek
first the kingdom and all else will be added"—seek first that consciousness
in which you understand that the kingdom is within;
seek first that belief that knows you can move any mountain; seek first
from the depths of the divine vortex where your dreams perpetually evolve
out of your own making; seek first what no man can tear asunder; seek
first what no appearances of flesh can defy; seek first what no devil of your
own making can limit; seek first the knowledge that you are gods.*

*This Son of mine, when he was but 12 years old he taught men 5 times
his age at the Temple.*
*Like the brown girl whose consciousness gave birth to him, he knew the
Truth before he was born, and he came to remind you, he came to refresh
you, he came to covenant with you, he came to restore you, he came to
lift you out of your self-imposed shackles, he came to heal you, he came to
anoint you, he came to give you back your sight.*

*This is the Son who turned water into wine. He told me it was not yet
time, but at my gentle urging, he revealed the power inherent in all of
us to change the ordinary into the extraordinary. This is the Son who
destroyed the demons. When he called to them, they answered and rather
than feel his wrath, they ran into the sea
and drowned in the bodies of swine.*

ॐ⊷

Release Your Demons

Clean Up Your Act

This is the season to clean the cracks of every small corner that you've been hiding in, and draw the living water from the sweetness of your own well.

☙❧

Listen up my daughter. Let's get real about the hatred and resentment for yourself that sometimes leaks out to your sisters and to others. Jealousy and spite is one of several demons that you must release from your lives. The only way that you can cleanse what you don't need in your life is to take an honest inventory of what's there. As my beloved son Jesus taught, you should have so much integrity that if your right eye causes you to sin, you must gouge it out and throw it away and if your right hand causes you to sin, you must cut it off and throw it away (Matthew 5:29-30).

It takes a lot to cut off your hand or pluck out your eye, and fortunately, it's not required that you do that in the physical realm. But you must do the work. Do as much as you can to clean up your act. Only then, do you even begin to see the blessings behind the door upon which your heart knocks. You have to dig well beyond the appearances of the life you lead to remove all of the complex lies that you hide in. The Seventh Commandment says, you shall not commit adultery. A better way of saying this commandment is not just that you cannot cheat on others but that you must not cheat yourself. If you are lying to others, you are lying to yourself. If you are cheating yourself, you are not being your best nor are you attracting the best relationships and experiences to you.

Anytime you are not being honest and true to yourself, you are committing adultery. Even if you are faithful to your spouse in the physical sense, you are cheating your spouse and yourself if you don't want to be in the marriage, but you don't have the courage to leave. Anytime you are dishonest, you are committing adultery because you are cheating yourself by living a lie. Jesus confronted everyone with their lies when he told the crowd at the Mount of Olives, let he who has no sin cast the first stone (John 8:7).

Not a single one of you is perfect. All of you have lied at one time or another. All of you have cheated. All of you have sinned. Cleaning your house does not permit finger-pointing, unless it is at yourself. Each person on the Mount of Olives who had condemned the woman scorned disappeared when Jesus added the requirement that only those who had no sin could stone her. Each person left one by one, beginning with the oldest even to the last. No one was spared.

Cleaning your house means that you release your demons, let go of the past, step away from the toxicity that you used to have and move forward in the divine energy of renewed commitment. Jesus said, go and sin no more (John 8:11). How exactly do you do that? When you look at where you are, it may seem overwhelming. *First*, you can start with the physical stuff. You can throw away or give away the papers, the boxes, the files, the clothes, and other stuff that you no longer need—in order to make room for the new. When you do this simple physical task, you open spaces in your consciousness to receive my good.

Second, you can forgive the people, the situations and the circumstances that you have been holding onto. Sometimes you can't do this part alone. So pray to me, and I will do the work. I will do the heavy-lifting of disappointments, pain and remorse. This requires you to stop hanging on to crutches and stop languishing in the belief that you are less than God's anointed. Deep down inside, you are aware of the relationships that no longer serve your highest good, that are filled with jealousy and gossip and hatred. All you have to do is release them. Center yourself in me as the place where they cannot exist, a place cleansed of your own bitterness and frustration, one where you have released whatever and who-ever was not supportive of your higher good and greater purpose. Even those you thought were friends must be released when they will not support your success.

Third, you have to cleanse the consciousness and conduct that causes you to cheat yourself out of being the divine creation that you are. This is even more difficult than ending your misconduct itself. In order to cast out the old hang-ups, fears and doubts, you have to first identify them; and then you have to be courageous enough to let them go. You have to be honest with yourself about what causes you to fall short of what you want to accomplish in your life. You have to be honest about what you need to do in order to demonstrate the power that you are blessed with.

Beloved, this is your stuff that I need you to work through me to clean up. These are your demons. They don't belong to anyone else. As long as you have them, you will experience strife. As long as you and others have them, there will be hatred in the world. This is not a seasonal but an ongoing process of self-examination and self-discovery. If you want to release your demons, you can't just wallow in your mess. At some point, you've got to let your stuff— the regenerative part of life that uproots and restructures—go so that you can be blessed with something new.

Paul said "I die every day" (1st Corinthians 15:31), teaching you that the need to change, to deconstruct, to reinvent, to tear the feathers from your own wings and allow some aspect of you to be destroyed—is tantamount to the resurrection that you need to shed the old so that you can make way for the new. You sometimes need to strip down to your bare essentials so that you can feel the ease of simplicity in everything that you do. For you, that may mean doing nothing, moving slowly, watching carefully, listening deeply, moving quietly, waiting patiently, or releasing gracefully. It's not a time of mourning either; it's a time of allowing every aspect of who you are to change.

It's not what you harvest that matters, but what you've learned through sowing, pruning, weeding and mulching. If you do the necessary cleaning, you can release the stuff that you don't need and create a more fertile space to honor whatever remains. You can look at yourself with new eyes and a brand new possibility of salvation—not based on who you once were, but who you are beneath your stuff.

᠅

ক্ক

FROM HER SCROLL CALLED FREEDOM

Manna stood on the precipice of time—
somewhere lodged between now and forever, somewhere in the midst of the
old and the new, somehow connected between beginnings and endings,
somehow carrying the sweetness of breath and energy and love—as care-
fully as the last refrain of a song that just gets better and better, and no
one wants it to end, so they just keep playing it.

Manna seemed no more than a dribble of sweat off the wisp of her honey
brown twists of hair soft and full and glistening with sun. Fearlessly, her
powerful eyes focused with precision—past into present into then and
later, into space where no human eye could see.
Wherever she wanted to be, she was.
Whatever she wanted to answer, she did.
Whenever she wanted to listen, she heard.
However, she wanted to touch, she reached.
Her caramel peanut butter latte, honey lemon crème, chocolate berry, red
clay, cinnamon copper brown skin was a reminder of who she was, but
not really because she changed hues as easily as the sun—depending upon
where she recreated herself in a universe of decisions.

Her choices were always dancing with joy,
always forever singing,
always with the oneness of time,
always clapping out peace,
always being born again.

ক্ক

I am the Only Freedom
that You Need

Dance on the breaths of sunshine.
Pull on the joy of heaven.
Dangle loosely from giving arms.
Beat out a new rhythm of freedom.
Find your stride.
Allow faith to ride again.
Let your soul run deep like the rivers.

৵৽৵

The book of Exodus teaches you that after the Israelites left Egypt, Moses climbed Mt. Sinai, and I appeared to him from the mountaintop and gave him Ten Commandments. Moses is a Hebrew word that means drawing out. Metaphysically, Moses means salvation. Moses was not just drawn out of the water and saved as an infant; he did not just *draw* the Israelites out of slavery and lead them to freedom; he released them from the slavery of negativity and led them to a consciousness of liberation.

When Moses went to the mountaintop, he rose in consciousness. He climbed in his prayer. He climbed in his meditation. He climbed in his affirmations. He climbed in his studies of truth. He climbed in his belief. He climbed in his faith, and he saw God. He was enlightened with divine principle, which gave him eternal truth.

The commandments are more rules of self-empowerment than they are restrictions on your life. They serve as a guide as to what you should do to stay centered in your divine path. The first one is the most important. I tell Moses to tell the Israelites "I am the Lord thy God, which have brought you out of the land of Egypt, out of bondage. You shall have no other gods before me."

This "I AM" principle is not saying that you owe me because I liberated you, but that in order to maintain your liberation, you can put nothing before me. I am the only source of your deliverance. When you realize the I AM as the God in you, nothing will have the power to enslave you.

Salvation isn't just saying that you acknowledge Jesus Christ as Lord and Savior. If you put the economy first, politics first, doubt first, reality shows first, old lovers first, jobs first, and even that old ugly, time-draining stuff from the past first, you aren't putting me first. I am the Alpha and the Omega, the first and the last; nothing and no one comes before me.

The Psalmist says, be still and know that I AM God. Be still and know that the most important communion in your life is your personal relationship with me—the God in you. When you know, believe, and center in the One Principle and Power of God, nothing can contain you. The shackles have to come off; the wilderness wandering has to end; the light at the end of the tunnel has to shine; the way *out of no way* has to open up.

Mary, Mary sings it well when they sing "It's the God in me!" Put nothing else before that realization. Your power is not the devil. It's not Satan. Your power is the God in you. Your power is not fear of the future; it's not fear of the past; it's not fear of what you can do; it's not worry about what you can't do. Your power is the God in you. The God in you prays and moves her feet. The God in you knows that all things come together for your greatest good.

I—the God in you—will rescue you from the river of abandonment, draw you out of the water of fear, allow you to leap—knowing that the net will appear, and crown you with victory before your race has begun. You see Beloved, the God in you is the only God there is—always and forever leading you out of the bondage of appearances to the freedom of simply being remarkable.

∂∽∾

ҩ๏ख़

FROM HER SCROLL CALLED FREEDOM

The truth had been all but forgotten.
No one was in the flesh who was there at the beginning. The universe was
their womb,
and their womb was the universe.
They could no longer look in the mirror,
and see that they were made in
Love's image and her likeness.
They could no longer remember the stories whose legacies were repeated
long before words.
She was one of millions of brown girls who were always left out—who did
not realize that she was the origin of all that was good—did not know
who she once was, she always would be.
Each new beginning found her whole:
pure, graceful, dynamic, blessed,
even after Hagar was raped;
even after the Romans fed her to the lions;
even after she was dragged through the middle passage; even after she was
paraded naked in a cage:
even after she worked America's fields and nursed her babies; even after
she helped her people escape to freedom—voiceless and faceless again.
She found herself lost in that gap of time between now and always—an
invisible brown girl, in whose nothingness, she was everything.

ҩ๏ख़

You Shall Not Want

love created the wings
of unlimited possibility.
a single word lifted from a universe
of endless nobility.

first delivered in spaces of breath
dancing between time
and then blown.
first whispered on lips of freedom
claiming glory now
and then gone.
first spun across centuries where
illumination dug deep
and then shone.
first pulling vision past pain where
brown girls found their own spirit
and then atoned.

༄

The Psalmist says, "the Lord is my Shepherd, I shall not want." How many times have you read that passage from the 23rd Psalm and never paid attention to its meaning? This single line is one of the most powerful affirmations there is. It means that I am your shepherd. It means that the divine vibrations that I express as you, the indwelling Christ consciousness in which you are reborn, the Holy Spirit—which lives in you, guides you, comforts you, and teaches you, is your shepherd. It means that I am always present, always constant, always watching over you, always making sure that you are protected, that you are fed, that no danger or harm comes near you. But most importantly, it means that because you live and move and have your being in infinite source, you have everything that you need. It means that there is no limit to my good.

I am always blessing you, always watching over you, always embracing you, always empowering you. You need to learn to see beyond your physical eyes. I am the substance, the catalyst, the creativity from which all life springs and all ideas evolve. You cannot even begin to imagine my greatness and the abundance of my Kingdom that is always available to you.

I am greater than miracles. I am greater than desire. Your difficulties arise when you believe that you are separate from the power that I give you. Pray with me. Meditate with me. Sit with me, and I will bless you with the opportunities that you need, the people who will help you, and the divine ideas that will bless you.

I am your shepherd, providing you with the ability to create good for not only yourself but to be a constant blessing, inspiration, and resource to others. Spirit is always leading you to the pasture of opportunity…if you listen. If you need a teacher, I am there. If you need a client, I will send them. If you need an answer, I will give one. If you need discernment, I will shepherd you through what you need to do.

No matter what you are up against, no matter what the appearances look like, no matter what the threat—it better *be*ware because I am with you: the Good Shepherd, the Infinite Power, the Almighty, the One who says that the battle is mine, the One who says touch not my anointed and do my prophets no harm, the One who teaches that all you have to do is believe. Your weapon is faith in me.

I have a rod and a staff that you can lean on: the right person who just shows up and says, I will do this for you, the closed sign doors that just open, the towering wall that is removed, the difficult passage that opens a way out of no way.

I will bless you from the top of your heads to the bottom of your feet. The good will flow to you from so many different directions that you cannot even begin to imagine what will be in store for you. The highways and the byways will just pour, and rain down blessings on you because—as the song goes—your "God is a good God." There is nothing that you will need.

ಹಿ ⊷

FROM HER SCROLL CALLED FREEDOM

*How could a fat brown baby remind them of all that God is? How could
a fat brown baby be the I AM of her being? How could she know that our
good is right where we are? How could she be the living manifestation of
all that is holy and pure?
How could she be the Yes! answer to all of her prayers?
Because she was born from a line of gods sprang forth from the oldest
brown girl, mother of all humanity—older than Eve's mother,
older than dirt, older than time.
It's just that she remembered
what we have long forgotten.
She carried a resounding YES! in her heart
and was bound to it in her soul.
She knew—YES! I can do all things
through the Spirit within me.
YES! I can surrender the inexhaustible
supply of the universe.
YES! I can run the race and not grow weary.
YES! I can move mountains
with the faith of a mustard seed.
YES! I can leap and the net will appear.
YES! I can do even greater things than Jesus.
YES! I am more than
my humanness can even imagine.
YES! I am the kingdom of heaven
giving way to infinite abundance.
YES! I am the unlimited love that you need to step into. YES! I am the
greater wholeness
always seeking expression.*

ಹಿ ⊷

I am the Road You Must Take

oh, when the unanswered prayer seeks.
oh, when the tongues of angels speak.
oh, when the rhythms sway to their own beats.
oh, when the holy ghost shouts at its peak.
oh, when the testimony of joy leaks.

mustard seeds of faith will blend
as ageless grains of time descend.
and spirits moving will transcend
as truth surrenders to the wind.

oh, as truth
rides gloriously in the wind.
ॐ᛫

You will reach that crossroad when you must make a choice, a decision to move in the right direction, a commitment to do what is consistent with what you want to accomplish, a willingness to travel the unbeaten path. The question becomes: Are you courageous enough, strong enough, enlightened enough to take the least traveled road through the wilderness? Are you strong enough to take the road of faith and trust and belief in me? The spiritual path will make an incredible difference and it will require sacrifice. It will require courage and consistency. But the rewards will be better than any other course.

When you decide to take a spiritual path—a life where you choose to do what's necessary to stay tuned in to me, you may find yourself alone. You may find yourself doing what's unpopular. You may even find yourself having to let go of some relationships. You will definitely have to release certain habits or activities—not because I require it, but because it will be inconsistent with the new you.

You have to decide who it is that you really want to be, what it is that you really want to do. Do you want to be extraordinary or common? Do you want to change your life or keep doing the same old same old? You will have to take responsibility for yourself. You will not be able to point the finger. You will not be able to keep blaming other people for wrong turns, delays, or new directions. You will have to venture out beyond your comfort zone. But you will find, as my beloved Jesus said, the gate will be narrow and the way is hard—but you will be among the few who find it (Matt. 7:14).

ॐ∽ॐ
FROM HER SCROLL CALLED FREEDOM

She had a funny way of looking into your soul.
She rubbed her wet fingers across your face.
She understood all languages but spoke none.
She knew all walks but her steps were uneven.
She could lift all burdens but her hands always moved. She hated prayers pronounced in perfect diction because they don't require the right words, only the right intent. She didn't have a big hat or matching gloves or an "Amen" prophetic enough to swing low in anybody's sweet chariot.

ॐ∽ॐ

The Time is Now

Brown girls uplift each other as women,
celebrating their victory as gods.
Their Mother God is here.
Their Father God is here.
The ancestors who put flesh on their bones,
hope in their hearts,
and love in their souls are here.

The time for your transformation is here. I am here to pull you through it. I am here to help you realize the benefit of surrender. There is no need to wait for a 9/11 or for some catastrophic event to take place in order for you to commit to my Spirit. You don't need to wait to experience the Kingdom of Heaven. Jesus teaches you that it is here and now.

The word "heaven" used in the Bible means expanding. Your dreams, goals, commitment to doing what Spirit has called you to do is part of your expansion. You expand by releasing lack, frustration and despair and believing instead in the omnipotence, omniscience and omnipresence of Spirit in you.

No matter what is before you in the flesh, you cannot forsake me. As Confucius says, great things have no fear of time. Everything is in perfect divine order. Whatever you need, whatever you long for is manifesting when it is supposed to. You are in your right time, at your right place. My substance is everywhere present in you and as you in all of your beauty and your strength and your sassiness and your sophistication and your charm. If you don't recognize me, you are always going to be missing something. Grab a hold a me now, right now—while the time is right. I am your true vine. I am your unlimited source. I am your bread from heaven. I am your manna.

Don't confuse me with the channels that I use to show you your good. I bless you in a multitude of ways. You lost your job? So what. You lost that opportunity you had staked your hope in? So what. I am trying to make you realize that there is something better in store! I am trying to make you aim higher than before. You don't need fortune tellers to forecast your future because I am co-creating as you. Instead, you can predict what you have in store for the future.

You can wear the biggest hat, hold the most prestigious position, and kneel in a temple made of pure gold, but it means nothing if you don't recognize the kingdom within you. The time to move away from appearances is now. The time to move away from confusion is now. The time to move forward as a full expression of Spirit is now.

I challenge you to start on the road that makes a difference by looking at yourself in the mirror and telling yourself how much you love you just the way you are. If you don't love yourself, then no matter what road you take, you will be lost. There is so much in you that wants to be and needs to be loved. But part of loving who you are is being honest about what you need to do to be your best. Ask yourself: How can I feel even better about myself? How can I slowly begin to take the steps that make me appreciate who I am? How can I slow down long enough to connect with the Divine Source that will lead me in the right direction? How can I enjoy each aspect of living and moving and being as part of the seamless energy that makes me uniquely me? How can I be about my business—without worrying about what anyone else thinks? How can I trust the love leading me—from my own heart?

When you begin to see the truth for yourself—that you hold the map to the best path, and you can follow your own faith to the kingdom of heaven—you will find that place where all of the power, all of the peace, all of the joy that you need is already expanding. Trust me, and allow heaven to expand in you. There is no need to wait for a new season, the time is now.

ॐ

FROM HER SCROLL CALLED CREATION

If you are captive to the ordinary, to the mundane, to the mediocre, to shadows of dreams that carry you to and fro as though you were a slave to space and time,
If you live a meager existence that realizes you were born to create but satisfies itself with less,
If you are struggling in the drama of someone else's hell and cannot seem to reach the door of your own awakening, repeating the same mistakes as though the treadmill of discontent is your journey,
If you are tied to the belief that someone else is Love, and you pray for him to do what
you have the power to manifest,
If you are locked in a consciousness that fails to realize it is a miracle of its own making,
If you are tip-toeing around truth that you are creator of everything in your midst,
If you are losing a race because as you press forward each lap moves you farther from the finish line,
then listen up, you who are the daughters and the sons of Love, you who were breathed from spirit and shaped from mother earth, you whose dreams were born in the rising sun and spun through the glorious stars:
You are more than you could ever imagine.
You are heirs to the throne.
Listen. You can hear your legacy in the wind.

ॐ

You Have Nothing to Fear

Plant hallelujah shouts, sow love seeds, reap Detroit beats, send sweet
magic, build faith rocks, deliver answered prayers, find sunny days.
Trust that blessings will come,
and dreams will be realized.
Have nothing to fear.

৯৯৯

You have nothing to fear. I cannot say this enough because I know that you must center yourself in this truth everyday—the truth that you are always supplied, always blessed, always anointed, always lifted, always protected, always spared, always delivered, always healed, always part of my infinite flow of divine substance. Not only are you blessed by my grace but also by my power. Victory is the ground upon which you stand.

I am the glorious foundation of all existence, the rock of all salvation, the path of all triumph. I will say it again: I am more than you could ever imagine God to be—more than the economy, more than a stimulus plan, more than a toxic derivative, more than a job. I am the divine surplus—always giving, always forming, always molding, always shaping, always rewarding, always liberating. I give you permission to laugh at life. You have nothing to fear.

Move out of your comfort zone and do what I have called you to do. Embrace all of the good that I offer you. Laugh at yourself recreating you.

I will open new doors. I will inspire new ideas. I will watch as you dance into and leap inside my realm of infinite possibilities. You can laugh at what appears difficult because with me, there is only success. You can laugh at your life, and in your laughter, embrace each moment with endless kisses and poems, hugs and twitters, stories and songs. In your laughter, you can let go of anything negative that you might have been holding onto and anyone. In your laughter, you can radiate new joy, solve new equations and fulfill new prophecies with power and vision. Laugh at whatever someone meant for evil because I mean everything for your good. Laugh at what you used to do because I will help you to put the past behind you—and do what you need to do. Laugh at what you must do because it now flows to you with ease. In your laughter, find my breath; breathe in my Aum, the I AM; reflect my love; attract my good; see the reflection of me—staring back at you, realizing that you are not afraid anymore. You are marvelous and magnificent, energetic and enlightened, prosperous and poised. Yes, you radiate the simple sweetness of a plain brown girl—not one bit sad or one bit worried—but completely aware that you are made in my image and likeness.

☙❧

FROM HER SCROLL CALLED FREEDOM

Aum was the deliverance that sounded the depths of the divine, that confounded the rays of the sun, that surrounded the galaxies of the universe. Aum, a single continuous sound—AUMMMMMMM, was all it took.

☙❧

Live in the Now

Open each season carefully. Dance inside its endless possibilities. Savor a generous slice of its divine ideas. Step gently on the waters of its conviction. Witness in it your own magic, your own miracle, your own inevitable creation.

೧~ல

Regardless of where you are or what you might be experiencing, live in the now. No matter what you are growing through, there really is no space to be in other than the present moment. Don't waste all of your time dwelling in the past. Release the past. Whatever took place years ago, months ago, a week ago, a day ago, even a minute ago—no longer exists. Now is the only thing that matters. I AM always power in you.

The thoughts that you think now are what create your present moment and give way to what you want to experience. So many of you limit yourselves by the past. You define yourselves based on the environment in which you grew up as a child—even though you may not have seen or experienced that environment in ten, twenty, thirty, forty, fifty, or even sixty years. You limit yourselves to what someone says about you in the past, to what you did in the past, or even to what you did not accomplish in the past. You are emotionally drained from relationships that have long been over. You feel trapped by mistakes made months or even years ago. But you must not only forgive others, you must forgive yourselves. The only way to move forward to accomplish your desires is to forgive, to release, to let go of the past.

The most liberating experience that you can have is the realization that in this moment, you are brand new. In this moment, you are whole, healed, spectacular, and awesome. In this moment, you release everyone who you believe did you wrong; you bless them and let them go. In this moment, you take responsibility for whatever it is that you want to create in your life. In this moment, you release the illness, the pain, the frustration, the doubt, the animosity, the fear—whatever limitations you have been holding onto, and you breathe in the breath of new possibilities, new hopes, new dreams, new beliefs, new experiences. If you could for one second, here and now, really know that I am you—you would change your life forever.

❧❧

FROM HER SCROLL CALLED FREEDOM

Aum was born when the single breath all of the symbols revealed in Revelation, pointed to the simple truth of Oneness, the illumined spirit of all humanity, united as God without a single shred of separation. AUMM-MMMMM. I am here, she said in the mosque. No, I am here, she said in the temple. I am here, she said in the church pew. No, I am here she said at the Buddhist chime. I am here, she said through the Hindu yogi. No, I am here, she said at the cross. I am here, she said at the medicine wheel when the smell of sage filled the air. No, I am here, she said at the Baptist revival. I am everywhere that you intend me to be.

❧❧

Tell a New Story

෪෬

who will discover
the bones of the plain brown girl
whose skull is as old as time
buried deep in the recesses
of prayers long forgotten

older than Lucy
older than Eve's mother
older than dirt

who will look long enough
into her empty sockets

who will dare to see themselves
gazing there.

who will find the courage to lift their legacy
out of the realm of the forgotten,
and speak the truth once again.

not that we are looking for God,
but oh, that we
have found her.

෪෬

See with a New Light

She sings melodies from psalms
only she can hum,
Galilee on her tongue,
speaking from that city on a hill,
singing "this 'lil light of mine—
I'm gon' let it shine."

❧❧

Many of you have been telling the same stories for so long that you no longer know truth from fiction. You have no idea who you really are in the Spirit as opposed to who you are in the flesh. The "you" who was abused, neglected, rejected or condemned in the past—was given a starring role in your life story, while the real you took a back seat. I am here—not to undermine but to free you from your past. Stop holding up your past like a mirror. It impairs your ability to see who you are. The only way that you are going to see me reflected in your image and likeness is to free yourself from the past, and tell a new story. Throw away the regret and the pain and the hurt that has been passing for a life and see yourself with a new light.

You are not who you were yesterday. Let me say that again, the you who just opened this book is not the "you" who did all of the things that you believe held you back from accomplishing your goals. You are different. You are reborn. You are free. Begin to see yourself with a new light.

Read the Book of Matthew, Chapter 6, Verse 22. It says that the light of the body is the eye: if therefore your eye is single, your whole body will be full of light. It is providing you with a lens through which you can see all of the experiences that I have given you with a new insight. What you see in the flesh is around you, but it is not of you. Jesus tried to explain this when he said, "I am not of this world" (John 8:23). Spirit is the only thing that matters. Look only to me. Seek first my kingdom. Wait upon me, and I will heal your wounds and allow you to move forward with them as a blessing rather than a hindrance.

If you see with a new light, you will know that I am in the midst of everything and everyone, and you will be able to discern my presence. But you can't have it both ways. You can't see me half the time and get stuck in a rut the other time. Your eye must be single and focused on me. Otherwise, you will multiply your errors, lose your perspective, and do foolish things. You will say what you later regret. You will waste time that could have been well spent in a more focused, productive, enjoyable fashion. You will act out of negative emotions rather than with confidence and purpose.

When you fail to keep your focus on Spirit, you will find yourselves like that beggar on the roadside—blinded by your lack of faith. Remember what Jesus told the blind man? Jesus said your faith has made you whole. The blind man's faith had made him see. If your eye is single, your whole body shall be full of light. But if you are not centered in my light, your direction, your intuition, your divine compass will be off, and you will find ourselves stumbling in the darkness. Without my light, it's difficult to tell a new story for yourself because you cannot see who you really are.

Spirit is the light that unifies you in consciousness and centers you in peace, clarity, creativity, joy, and abundance. Only when you are centered in my light do you realize your oneness with the entire universe. If you achieve this going forward, you will not be limited the way that you were in the past. You will realize that the heartache or the pain that you experienced can be released and you can stop re-living it. You can begin to recreate who you want to be rather than who you used to be.

One way of centering in my presence is through the third eye, which can be accessed by focusing on the center of your forehead. The pineal gland—located in the brain behind the eyes—is said to be the physical entry of spiritual enlightenment, also known as the gateway to faith. It is the home of higher consciousness, healing power, and psychic perception. When you practice looking deeply into your third eye, you will behold my light emanating from infinite source, what many of you call a cosmic vibration. When you are centered in this divine light, you can be even more open to my presence—beyond words and thoughts. When you focus through your spiritual eye, your inner eye, your third eye on my presence, your entire being—mind, body and soul—will be filled with light. This is the energy and the concentration that will also build and develop your faith—so that you won't have to spend a long period in tapping in or tuning in to me. With a single eye directed to divine source, you will be catapulted beyond your same old story and be able to walk by faith in me.

ॐ ॐ

FROM HER SCROLL CALLED CREATION

It is said that a brown girl named Grace
rose from the soil
where the garden once sat
and snakes spoke boldly to Africans
eating deliciousness and strength from the vines
of their earth mother's long fingers.

The firstborn was a brown girl more incredible than a saint, who would
give birth to generations after generations of lives.

Her Holy Spirit is always in our midst, guiding us through seasons yet
to come and generations unborn, unfolding the story of beginnings in the
wind, teaching us to know that the end always leads back to itself.

ॐ ॐ

Move with a New Courage

I AM greater than you could ever imagine.
I can walk through the fire,
cut to the chase,
rise to the occasion.

I never lose, never miss, never falter.

☙❧

Part of telling your new story requires you to move with new courage in mind, body and soul. Courage is mental strength. Without it, you will be weak regardless of how strong you are physically. The Psalmist asks, if the Lord is the Strength of my life, of whom and what shall I be afraid? (Psalm 27) This not only means that I am able to do something for you, it also means that you are able to feel my strength in you. You worry less. You take more chances. You are more confident. You trust me. You move forward, knowing that you can accomplish whatever you set out to do.

You have nothing to fear with me by your side. You reflect me as you rise to any occasion. You do not hesitate to tap my power because you trust that I am always in your midst. But we have to be on one accord. I can't arm you and defend you and protect you if you aren't listening to me. I will give you all of the strength that you need. When you stand on my shoulders, your spiritual roots will reach down to the belly of the earth—without stopping there. You will know that the entire universe girds you with a strength and a power that never loses its connection. You will stand on your own two feet, stand up for yourself, and stand up for what you believe in with renewed courage and conviction.

You can see this spiritual courage in the story of David and Goliath. Goliath represents physical strength and prowess. Goliath is what you see in the flesh—the circumstances that appear so much greater than you. In the physical realm, if you judge by appearances, you believe that you cannot overcome what is bigger than you. But when you move forth with me and thus with a new courage, you can put on a new self, one that has the courage, the *spiritual strength* to fight the good fight. When you decide to be one with me and move forward with me as your helmet and armor and javelin and sword—you will have all the protection that you need.

I'm not telling you to do something foolish—not to exercise common sense in terms of personal safety. But I am telling you to be girded in me, girded in the kingdom of God in you—and you will have the foresight and the ability and the protection to win any battle. Look at David, who came forward, as a boy. You have to contrast David—the small and seemingly insignificant aspects of your own lives—with the big issues of doubt and fear that you have—your Goliath of lack, Goliath of loss, Goliath of fear—and use the power of the "little" that you have. David was saying, I don't have a spear and I don't have a helmet. I don't even have a shield. But I've got my raggedly shepherd's cloth. I've got my staff. I've got my slingshot—that I have fashioned from a tree branch. I have the earth under my feet—and all that the earth is made of. But most importantly, I stand on the strength of Spirit—a love that is invincible, a power that never leaves me, a protector that can never be defeated.

As Goliath moved closer to attack him, David ran quickly toward the battle line to meet him. Without hesitation, David ran to face his adversary head on. He didn't have to be as big or as tall as Goliath because he stood on my shoulders. Reaching into his bag for one of the stones that he had gathered, David took it out and struck Goliath on the forehead. The stone sank into Goliath's forehead, and Goliath fell face down on the ground. Fear, doubt, lack and limitation were defeated in a single shot—by a kid and a slingshot.

David struck the center of those mental blockages on his path that seemed insurmountable. Goliath was struck in the center of his head—that part of his body connected to the pineal gland where the third eye of spiritual discernment could give him vision beyond flesh. It is easy to think of David and Goliath as separate beings, but as two parts of a whole, we see internal strength defeating external prowess. Nothing is powerful enough to block you from the attainment of your good. Be renewed in the knowledge that I am bigger than anything that you could ever imagine.

༅ ༅

FROM HER SCROLL CALLED CREATION

Her sister was Karma, who bore the children that became the twelve tribes of the world.

Karma begat Chinwendu, Chibuzo, Aliyah, Fumnanya, Azubuike, Chukwuemeka, Sanjit, Bogani, Chianaka, Anuli, Asim, and Chinweuba.

Each one of Karma's children begat twelve children, including Aliyah, who begat Amara, Abha, Sati, Kama, Oz, Anish, Vijaya, Rei, Zyri, Dayo, Ananita, and Eniola.

Each Aliyah's children begat twelve children, including Sati, who begat Pran, Dara, Tora, Ife, Zuberi, Hadas, Olufemi, Yaffe, Kanti, Aliza, Adel, and Rahima.

Each one of Sati's children begat twelve children, including Tora, who begat Lesedi, Dipika, Chingere's, Fumnanya, Zuberi, Anish, Amarachi, Kanti, Furaha, Manju, Khalid, and Aishwarya.

Each one of Tora's children begat twelve children, including Chingere, who begat Benjamin, Essie, Myrtle, Mazell, Jesse, Arthur, William, Jay, Plenie, Mae, Lena, and Shirley.

Each one of Chingere's children begat twelve children, including Myrtle, who begat Chi, Fern, Rose, Alice, Bianca, Esther, Sara, Wendy, Bernice, Zuri, Asim, and Acacia.

༅ ༅

Know with a New Understanding

Eve's mother
laughed at the beginning of time
let it pour into her
sweet brown soil
like fresh seed
heaving and groaning
and sighing
with the smell of thunder on her breath
her gurgling streams
wiggling free
like oceans bursting
from her shores
no sign of man yet
or beating drums
or wayward ships
or gin

just a plain brown girl
who had no name for God,
but who could always
remember her mother.

ॐॐ

You can't tell a new story, if you don't understand the old one. You can't tell a new story if you don't understand me and know what I am available to express in and as you. A new story has nothing to do with the number of books you read or degrees you've attained. It's not about looking a certain way, or worshipping a certain way. It's the constant enlightenment that you receive when you know that I am the source of your wisdom.

Everything that you experience is here to teach you about your divine connection to me—to the universe—to the invisible life force that lives and breathes and has its being as you. Your new understanding reveals that wisdom has nothing to do with age. I give you the understanding that you need regardless of your age. In the Book of Luke, you learn that when Jesus was twelve years old, his parents found him in the temple courts, sitting among the teachers, his elders—who were amazed at his understanding.

Watch your babies. Don't you realize that an inner wisdom is guiding them, protecting them, watching over them, forming and shaping and informing them? Remember when there were a number of cases in the media where babies were falling or being pushed or dropped out of windows—and they were holding onto curtains and tree branches. None of them were harmed. They were breaking their own falls. Spirit—the presence of wisdom—the I AM that I AM is their constant, present source of guidance too.

You don't lose this connection to me as you grow older. It becomes even more profound, but you tend to stand in the way of it. You stop listening to yourself. You start ignoring my voice within you that tells you where to go and what to do and not to forget certain things. I am that inner wisdom that is here to break your fall, to save you, to give you life, to ease and make safe your path, to show you what you must do, to bring you out of despair, to feed you the manna that has never stopped falling, to open up infinite channels of your good.

With a new sense of your inner wisdom, you will make right decisions, remove the toxicity out from your life, soar higher than you've ever soared before. In the 3rd Proverb, Solomon says: "Trust in the Lord with all your heart and lean not on your own understanding; in all your ways acknowledge him, and he will make your paths straight." The him that Solomon refers to is not an old white man but the kingdom of God within you. When you trust my direction, you learn quickly the lessons you need to know, and your challenges become your greatest allies rather than your worse adversaries.

Mistakes are merely opportunities to grow wiser. Even betrayal is your teacher because it brings you back to honesty and forgiveness. Unfinished tasks will teach you closure and completion. Failures will teach you how to honor successes. Your greatest fears will reveal your true power and guide you to your lasting deliverance. I will make sure that you graduate from the accelerated program of being certain of who you are, of knowing your true value, of accepting all of you.

꒰ꔛ꒱

FROM HER SCROLL CALLED CREATION

Each one of Rose's children begat twelve children, including Mary, who begat Wilhemina, Natalie, Aakhu, Christina, Christiana, Najah, John, David, Marlon, Edward, Brenda, and Jesus.
Each one of Mary's children begat twelve children, including Aakhu, who begat Christopher, Donald, Camille, Gregory, Christa, Carla, Taylor, Franklin, Scott, Walter, Robert, and Sandra.

Each one of Aakhu's children begat twelve children, who begat twelve children, who begat twelve children, who begat twelve children, who begat twelve children, who begat twelve children, who begat twelve children, who begat twelve children, who begat twelve children, who begat twelve children, who begat twelve children, including Camille, who begat Beth, Patricia, Elizabeth, Marilyn, Catherine, Terrie, Patrick, Rhonda, Wendy, Azalia, Denzell, and Angelina.

꒰ꔛ꒱

Create with a New Power

Harvest the new fruit of autumn's imagination.
Dance in the splendor of fresh winds.
Shake off whatever doesn't sit well with your soul.
Let it fall, in all of its many colors.

ॐॐ

Celebrating yourself allows you to create with a power that you've never created with before, a power that will permit you to demonstrate immediate change in your life. You always have the ability to choose but you usually fail to exercise it. You have the ability to choose to be well. You have the ability to choose to succeed. You have the ability to choose to be wealthy. You have the ability to choose to be strong. You have the ability to choose to be smart. You have the ability to choose to feel great about being great.

Your ability to choose does not discriminate. It is the divine right of each and every one of you. The book of Acts, Chapter 1, Verse 8, tells those of you who don't know that "you will receive power when the Holy Spirit comes on you." It doesn't say if you want power ask God for it—or better yet, go to God so God can be power for you. It doesn't say beg God, implore God, plead with God, cry out to God for power. Jesus said you will receive power when YOU ARE OPEN AND RECEPTIVE TO ABSOLUTE GOOD—WHEN the Holy Spirit comes upon you.

Second Timothy reiterates in Chapter 1, Verse 7, that "God did not give us a spirit of timidity or fear; but a spirit of power...." The sooner you recognize your power, the sooner you accomplish your goals, the sooner you step up to the plate and do what you were called here in this lifetime to do—the sooner you will make the world a better place, evolve into a completely new existence and recognize the God that you are. You are the Creator of your own reality. You create what you want to create—and you don't have to be realistic. There is no such thing as "realistic" when you are talking about Spirit—the power of the universe.

Just listening to me is pure power. Listening to the silence is one of the most powerful things that you can do to change your life. In the silence, you don't limit yourself to human nature; you move beyond thoughts to experience the essence of Spirit. In the silence, you feel your divine connection with a source that is more powerful than what you see in the flesh. When you still yourself in the silence, your intuition is sharper. You hear what I am directing you to do. The answers that you need come to you. You are guided to make the best decisions. You are calmer. You are more peaceful. You are centered in my grace.

Your thought is your power giving way to form. Thoughts register in your consciousness as vibrations. They don't just sit in your head; they move through the universe like rockets—targeting what you want them to hit, planting the seeds of what you want to see grow—molding and shaping your ideas—the ideas that the universe gives you. You can choose your thoughts. Power is the ability to choose your thoughts. Let that resonant deep within you that you can change your thoughts right now. You need to decide what you want to experience in your life.

There is power in your words. Everyday declare what you want in your life. Wake up and declare it. Go to bed and declare it. Stand up in your office and declare it. Look out your window and declare it. Walk down the street and declare it. Your words are where you take responsibility for what you want to see manifest in your life.

To the Dogon people in Africa, words are fertile. They contain the essence of life—the force of the creator travels through the breath of each spoken word. John said, in the beginning was the Word and the Word was God. The aborigines would say the tongue of Great Spirit resides in all things.

Power is your ability to choose to celebrate who you are and what contribution you can make to this beautiful existence that you call life. It gives you the honor to take charge of you. All you have to do is be willing to create your own story.

❧❧

FROM HER SCROLL CALLED CREATION

Each one of Camille's children begat twelve children, who begat twelve children, who begat twelve children, who begat twelve children, who begat twelve children, who begat twelve children, who begat twelve children, who begat twelve children, who begat twelve children, who begat twelve children, who begat twelve children, who begat twelve children, who begat twelve children, who begat twelve children, who begat twelve children, who begat twelve children, who begat twelve children, who begat twelve children, who begat twelve children, including Elizabeth, who begat Sheryl, Beverly, Manna, Zoe, Paige, Myreah, Eric, Joyce, Judy, Hope, Faith, and Dawn. Each one of Elizabeth's children begat twelve children, including Manna, who begat Obery, Dale, Devi, Edward, James, Peter, Jerome, Benjamin, Myrtle, Essie, Clara, and Lois. Each one of Manna's children begat twelve children, including Devi, who begat Louise, Sandra, Desire, Kenneth, James, Mary, Myrtle, Michael, Christa, Carla, Christopher, and Lois. Each one of Devi's children begat twelve children, including Desire, who begat Paulette, Mary, Hattie, Ti'Sha, Di'Maya, Damon, Keith, Ashley, Alta, Gregory, Donald, and Jerome. Each one of Desire's children begat twelve children, including Hattie, who begat Mable, Betty, Angelina, Dorothy, Rhonda, Fern, Scott, Taylor, Hicey, Myrtle, Christa, and Franklin. Each one of Hattie's children begat twelve children, including Angelina, who begat Thomas, Patrick, Anu, Lawrence, Goscelyn, Kervin, Paul, David, Marlon, Leslie, and Byron.

❧❧

Surrender with a New Will

If I need you to release your fears, will you open your eyes
and realize the strength of your own salvation?
Will you praise the divine creation that you are?
Will you kneel with me
at the altar of infinite possibilities?
Will you keep your promise
to be the blessing that you were born to be?

৵৶

You must have the power to create but also the humility to honor my will—God's will expressing in and as you. What are you being Spirit-led to do? Are you being obedient to your calling, your gifts, your talents? In John 5:30, my beloved Jesus says, I seek not my own will but the will of the Father who sent me. When you have a willing spirit, you don't have to worry, fret or despair because you flow with the infinite stream of all things working together for your good. Regardless of the appearances in the material world, it is the willing spirit that sustains you. It is not merely your desire but my will that moves you through your own mediocrity into the joy of your salvation; and the only way to experience this transformation is by surrendering to me.

It may seem as if you just don't have the time to surrender—you have so many things to do, so many tasks to occupy you. It is only when life kicks you in the shins that you start paying attention to what I tell you to do. But you don't have to suffer to appreciate the difference between being willing and being "willful." If there is something out of alignment with me, you need to be *willing* to correct it. If there is something that you are doing that is inconsistent with your integrity, you need to be *willing* to end it. I will give you the power to do what you need to do, as long as you are *willing*. You just need to be *willing* to allow me to bless you.

❧❧

FROM HER SCROLL CALLED FREEDOM

*We surrender to the understanding that we, of ourselves, can do nothing.
Spirit that does the work that we are called to do. With each new birth
and each new infusion of life breathing as us, we surrender to power of
the God in us, a power far greater than who we are—a power that knows
what we have need of—before we even ask.*

*We surrender—not by resisting change but by accepting all of the good
that the universe has in store for me. We surrender—not by drowning in
the self-pity of doubt but by being patient, by trusting that all things are
working together for our good in perfect, divine order.*

*We surrender—not by holding onto what once was but by releasing old
habits and patterns, by letting go of any criticism that we have of ourselves, by stepping out of the shackles of the past. We surrender—to the
knowledge that before we call, God will answer. We surrender every effort,
every attempt, every struggle—and we open our consciousness this day to
receive the kingdom of God.*

*We surrender every fear, every pain, every worry, every failure, every
guilt, every shame. We surrender every decision, every choice, every fork in
every path, knowing that God directs our course.*

❧❧

Heal with a New Wholeness

her brownness as fertile as the earth
never dies and is reborn
generations after generations of lives
want to bury her bones
but they just keep rising to the top

her holy spirit
always in our midst
guiding us through seasons yet to come
and generations unborn

ॐॐ

You cannot tell a new story unless you do it with health and wholeness. You have to listen to my guidance in every aspect of your life, including fitness. You must eat the foods that I make with the earth, rain, sun, shade, and what you call organic or natural resources. You cannot allow the temptations of man-engineered sugars and fats and chemicals to indulge you. I have already made the foods that you need—the ones that will give you strength, energy and vitality. You must eat clean, avoiding processed food like white or enriched starches. Eat the fruits, vegetables and grains that I have provided. You must drink plenty of water and get plenty of rest. You must weight-lift regularly to develop muscle mass and do cardio consistently each day. But to achieve the wholeness that will harmonize your body, mind and soul, you must center in me daily.

Everyone's body is different because I have made each one of you unique. But I will reveal to you what you need to do for your body type and fitness goals through the right teachers and trainers and resources. Don't be so quick to grab every manmade gimmick or supplement or prescription. If you listen, I will always guide you to the right source of information to stay whole. The real key to physical fitness is to put me first, which means that you must center in the kingdom of God within.

You say that you put me first, but I know that you don't. When I call you to pray with me in the morning, you roll over. When I tell you to slow down during your day, you talk on the phone, or send email, or gossip, or flirt, or turn on the television, or surf the net, or shop, or get your hair done—anything to avoid listening to me. You cannot change your outer experiences until you change your daily communion with me. Stop worshipping the idols of morning news, or morning coffee, or angry bosses—and center in my presence. I am always guiding you, always telling you the right way to go, the right way to achieve your goals, the right things to do to shine your light and experience your true greatness. Slow your roll. You are already in my hands, and in my heart, and in my soul. I love you like you can never imagine. I am here to re-connect you, to re-member your disconnected parts, to re-gather the fragments of your being so that you can really experience *all of that.* Yes, you are what you call—*all of that.*

You don't take the time for Spirit because you assume that centering in me has to be difficult. Whenever you pray, you only do it because you want something in particular. Then, you actually ignore me by speaking so loudly into your own clasped hands that you drown out the infinite channels of my guidance by trying to impose your will. But if you listened to me, I would give you answers before you even asked.

You say that you are aware of my presence. "To God be the glory" you say. "Amen" you say. "Hallelujah" you say. But then, you don't even see me in the air that you breathe and the space that you take up. I am not some place in the distance waiting to be called or begged or solicited. I am every aspect of who you are. When Paul says that you live and move and have your being in God, that means that there is no separation between all that you are and all that I am. Keep your mind stayed on me.

There are millions of ways to tap into and turn on my presence. But here is an easy way for you to walk in the newness of life. It takes less than five minutes. As soon as you wake up, sit up in your bed and immediately breathe in and breathe out, focusing on the breath of life as the infinite power of Spirit. Seek first the kingdom within your own consciousness, the awareness that the kingdom of God is the only power that there is, the only strength that there is, the only supply that there is, the only peace that there is, the only source that there is. Exercise your spiritual muscle of awareness by centering in the truth that is in me—which means in you, in the universe, in the Divine Mind, every problem is already solved, every challenge is already won, every appearance of disease is already healed. My good is not something that is postponed until tomorrow, I am blessing you and healing you in this instant.

If you haven't taken the time to center in a conscious awareness of my good, then you are not exercising one of the strongest muscles that you have. I know that sometimes you get completely overwhelmed by all of the decisions that you have to make, the priorities that you have to set, and the distractions you sometimes give your energy to. But Jesus said, if you need help, just ask. Ask and it shall be given. He said, I have come so that you may have life and may have it more abundantly, so just ask for what you need.

When you exercise your spiritual muscles by asking, you are not just receiving, you are simply becoming more receptive to giving your best. You open your consciousness to trust the universe and find perfect order and harmony in everything that you do because you have cleared the way for God's good to manifest through a consciousness that receives an unlimited supply of my good. How do we ask? There are as many ways as there are people. The most important thing to do is to trust me so much that you know what you need is already done. Speak your word of truth with the energy of power. Create an affirmation that you can say daily, at least one to four times each morning that not only asks but affirms that you have already received what you desire (*e.g.*, I am fit. I have a new job. My body is healed. My book is finished). It can be as long as you want, declaring that you already have the good that I am just waiting to give you. The words that you speak are powerful, as powerful as when I created the world that you live in. Remember, I SAID let there be light, and there was light.

Open your heart to accept my good. Stop choosing struggle and pain, and you won't experience it. Stop undermining and underestimating the gifts that I give to you. Look around and appreciate what I have placed on your path. You are good enough. I am tired of hearing you scream in churches that you are not worthy. You are worthy. You are better than the best. Stop saying poor me; you are a queen; you are an heir to my throne. Stop criticizing and condemning those who are living large; my house has many mansions. I have a place for you too—not just part of you, but all of you. I don't care if you wear a hat or gloves. But if you do, fill them with all of your grace and beauty. My love, my power, and my magnificence is available to everyone. Stop standing in the way of my gifts to you. I am trying to pour them through the windows of heaven and give you so many that you won't have room enough to store them.

Start anew. Right now, in this instant, start anew. And each day that you wake up, know that you are at a new beginning. Paul said, *I die daily* (1 Corinthians 15:31). Every day, every minute, every second, I will give you a clean slate. There is no need to carry past mistakes into each new moment of endless opportunity. There is no need to blame anyone. There is no need to feel guilt. Choose to align your movement in this universe with the divine guidance of pure love and absolute good. There is no need to suffer. Wear the world as a lose garment. Do not give your energy to gossip or confusion or despair. Take care of my business here and now, and I will take care of you.

இ–௧

ༀ

FROM HER SCROLL CALLED VICTORY

When she was ready, Aum didn't care where she came from nor where she arrived. She spun herself from the lips of Love and just surrendered. Love heard her whisper from a crack in the cosmos—filled with space and time and light. Love suddenly positioned all of the power that she was—and ignited the determination of a single breath—until the world heard Aum. She was a fragment of generations before her, who could ride the backs of any soul's salvation and be remembered. And without any effort, without any struggle, without any strain, without any pain, she was born: AUMMMMMM.

If you weren't listening, you wouldn't even know she was there. She came so quickly, so deliberate, so sure. If you didn't connect at the moment with the Holy Ghost, you may have simply found yourself, like so many others—mesmerized by her angelic presence. Aum was as strong as she was subtle. She was as vital as she was vested. She was as real as the water ran everywhere. "Here I AM," she screamed at the top of her lungs. "Here I AM," she ran deep in the longing of the world. "Here I AM," she vibrated, singing voices in tongues that she knew spoke in and as her. Here I AM.

ༀ

Love with a New Heart

the price she pays to be a savior,
sometimes muttering to herself.
her full lips quivering, her brown hands clean—
always handing out miracles.

there she was on the Sabbath,
working in that restless way of hers,
being everything that Love could ever imagine,

always answering,
whenever you knocked.

&‑&

I bless you with the power of regenerating love and by so do-ing, I ask that you love with every aspect of your new heart. Your new heart does not carry condemnation. Your new heart is only filled with love and its presence and its power. With a new heart beating as me, you will breathe love as your breath, love as your energy, love as the *me* that you exude, radiating exquisite beauty.

Your new heart will remind you of who you are. Your true roots are not of a place or a people; they are the energy out of which you were formed and made—and that energy is love. You are not limited; you can shape and mold and create out of any-thing that I give you.

Your new heart will not allow you to sit on the power that you are. That's what is creating the shake-up that you are experiencing in the physical realm right now. You have given your power away. Balance will not be restored until you love with a new heart—by using your ability to create, to manifest, to produce, to generate. The universe needs you.

I am not talking about romance. I am not talking about sex. I am not talking about the glitz and glamour of your exploitation of the gifts that I have given you. I am talking about the deep penetrating love that you must have for yourself, for your proper place in my kingdom. All of my children must stand hand-in-hand, side-by-side in the deliverance of this world. Only the harmony that you create will calm the raging seas and stop the global shifts, not to mention the pointless wars, the hunger, the health epidemics and the despair.

You have become complacent consumers—collectors of stuff—someone who just lives to purchase shoes and bags and designer wigs—forgetting your own callings. You have become lazy couch potatoes, zoned out internet surfers—greedy, selfish, and foolish enough to think that someone else should create for you and be loving for you—instead of tapping into the deepest powers of the universe that are always there—awaiting your instruction.

You are the love that you seek. You do exist to give without an agenda. Your love is secure. It has no need to scheme because it is not here to take—or to profit from anyone. You love is here to give.

But you have forgotten who gave you birth. You have forgotten your parents. You have forgotten that the world around you in the flesh is an illusion because you really dwell in one place, and that is in my heart. You are not separate from the infinite force and inexhaustible source of creative energy that called you into being to express the love that I AM—everywhere present and emanating from every pore and every divine vibration and every spirit-infused idea that gives shape to you. How can you refrain from being anything less than the love that created you. When you emanate in the powerful energy of all that Love is and allow yourself to be its co-creative channel of good—it will open way to all that you need, and all that you want, and all that you desire. When you love with a new heart, you will always be filled with my good.

When you shine your light as Love, the love that you seek CANNOT be withheld from you. If someone is bothering you, send love their way and watch what happens. If you have an injury or an ailment, send love its way and watch what happens. If you have a desire or a dream or a goal, keep sending love its way and watch what happens. If you want a divine partner, send love to the universe and the right person will manifest for you. Love cannot withhold from you what you need. Withholding your good defies the very nature of all that love is; it cannot happen. The good that you seek through the power of love will always be radiated back to you. Love cannot help but attract the right people, situations and circumstances to you.

If you love with a new heart, one that doesn't hold back, it will infuse you with a bliss that you have never felt before. Because you won't hold back, neither will I.

ॐ∽ॐ

FROM HER SCROLL CALLED CREATION

No matter what we see around us, we always have Love available within, demonstrating the good that is with us even in the rough times. Love will patch us up and mend us and lift us in the wind to experience seasons yet to come and generations unborn. Love is mother of us all and each one of us are her newborn babies suckling her deliverance. Love is also mother as us, a protection without boundaries, a shield without fear, a strength without separation from true source.
It was Love who took Myrtle to the square.
It was Love that showed Myrtle how to take her own body and use it to cover her daughter in the square.
It was Love oozing out of Myrtle that took the beating, no matter how many rocks came or who threw them.

The stones flew in the wind like the hard edges of hail balls and flew like unrestrained hatred. Love reminded Myrtle that each thrower would suffer the indignity and the hardship of his own transgression in lives to come. Love told Myrtle to tell Rose that she would have a chance to get it right and that she would run from these stones in many shapes until one day, she would be able to face them on her own. The stones might appear as earthquakes. They might appear as gossip and falsehoods. They might appear as disease and sores. They might appear as faces returning in the wind or bodiless men who come to claim their penalty. Tell her, tell Rose that the only way she will gain her freedom from the impossible is through Love.
Love is the only healer that there is.

ॐ∽ॐ

Persist with a New Determination

May you spin your jazz notes
off the shoulders that you stand on
and find rhythm in the quiet,
bringing the extraordinary to the imaginary
and the miracle to the sacred task,
the exquisite to the bare bones,
and the prophecy to the complete,
and the finished.

Oh Beloved,
be the goddess that you are,
and never, ever hold back.

➽ ✑

I love the story of the gold digger who gave up and sold his mining machinery to a junk man. The junk man was smart enough to hire a mining engineer, who calculated that the gold vein was just three feet away from where the drilling had stopped, which was exactly where the junk man found it. You tend to examine this story from the perspective of the gold miner who had abandoned his machinery. You believe that *"persist until you succeed"* is the only message of this story. But no one ever tells this story from the perspective of the junk man.

In John 4:37-38, Jesus told his disciples "the saying 'One sows and another reaps' is true. I sent you to reap what you have not worked for. Others have done the hard work, and you have reaped the benefits of their labor." You are really above creation's laws of cause and effect. If you are centered in me, you will reap without measure the infinite reward of my Spirit. Your soul need acquire nothing. All you have to do is remember what you already possess.

My desire to express through you is so great, you always reap more good than you sow. Jesus told his disciples in Matthew 9:37 that "[t]he harvest is plenty but the workers are few." At some point in your lives, you have stopped short of your true potential, but I will give you favor, so that in all things, at all times, you will have what you need. Beethoven failed at playing the violin and his music teacher called him hopeless as a composer, but he still reaped his harvest. Walt Disney was fired for lack of ideas and went bankrupt several times before he was able to build Disneyland, but he still reaped his harvest. Albert Einstein was described as mentally slow and could not get admitted to the Zurich Polytechnic School, but he still reaped his harvest. Michael Jordan was kicked off his high school basketball team, but he still reaped his harvest. My flow is constant.

The harvest is always in your midst. All you have to do is persist with a new determination, one that realizes that I am your only source. Tell a new story by realizing that this is your season, that you have the grace, that you have the favor to reap the benefits of a new consciousness in Spirit and through that glory to experience the true harvest. Walk in the realization of a new Spirit. Hold firmly to me—to the faith that you profess, without wavering. Walk into your season as more than just a witness. Be more than just a laborer. Be more than just a conqueror. Be prophetic in your vision, creative in your pursuits, innovative in your thinking, and grateful for the good that you were called to do. The true harvest is in the Spirit, where you will always reap the good that is inevitably yours.

ॐ◌ॐ

FROM HER SCROLL CALLED FREEDOM

I AM the one who sees souls igniting purpose.
I AM the one who lifts impossibilities beyond despair. I AM the one who
draws hope on wings of prayer.
I AM the one who believes…in the power that I AM.
If you find yourself pushed in a corner: all openings will reveal themselves
to you through me.
If you find yourself drowning in fear: all waves will become oceans of pure
possibility through me.
If you are lost in the shadow of despair: all roads leading to enlightenment
will move through me.
Look inside of your own clasped hands!
Acknowledge the longing in your own sweet heart.
Feel the freedom in your own surrender.
I am One with the Holy Ghost.
I am One with the single word meditation.
I am One with the dancer's leap, the musician's flow, the poet's rap, the
artist's vibe, the hip hop beating past convention into every place that you
began.
I am all that you are.

ॐ◌ॐ

Dance with a New Freedom

she wishes she could tell you the beginning
so that you would realize the end
is the glory of a song
and a dance
with heart and meaning,

the poetry of creation
always leading back to itself.

❧ ❧

Eric Butterworth was one of the great mystics of your time. He taught many Brown Girls and left many books and tapes as a lasting legacy. Before he made his transition, he was in a wheelchair. His voice had become so weak that those around him hung on to his every word. One of the last things that he said at a retreat in upstate New York was "I have no theology, I dance."

"I have no theology, I dance" means that you move with the Holy Spirit, move with the wisdom that there is no separation between all that you are and all that I am. You flow, you live, you laugh, you sing, you dance with a new understanding that you are unlimited in the Spirit, regardless of the appearances of the flesh. You are Spirit in movement.

You are not a religion, you are divine truth. You are constantly re-defining yourself because there is no limit to Spirit. In John 14:12, Jesus said, he who believes in me will do the works that I do also; and greater works than these will he do. When you dance in the Spirit, you realize that if things are not going the way that you want them to go; if you are not satisfied with the direction your life has taken; if you don't like the experiences that manifest in your life—you have the power to change them.

When you dance in the Spirit, you know that if patterns of negativity keep showing up in your life—such as disharmony, loneliness, pain, physical discomfort, financial insecurity, lack, worry, doubt—you can change them. You can wake up from your self-limiting thought and you can experience the ceaseless flow of good— and turn your life around. You can dance.

When you dance in the Spirit, you shake the dust off your feet. You bless the people who are not in accord with your greatest good, who do not support you and do what Spirit calls you to do. You dance in the joy of infinite possibility. You dance in the hope that you can create, grow, plant, deliver, empower, ignite, vote, rap, sing, write, dig, teach, sell, envision, tap, rescue, develop, uncover, realize something in your life that will heal the world of hatred, of doubt, of lack, of limitation.

The Psalmist says in the 8th Psalm, the 6th Verse, you have given him power over the works of your hands; you have put all things under his feet. You dance. No matter how unimportant, how trivial, how average, how unattractive, how old, how overweight, how unnecessary, how disabled you may seem to you, the dance that you do could not be done in quite the same way—without you doing it. You dance in the realization that you are my unique melody sung once—only once as you—one melody of Spirit singing itself into the continuum; and the music of the spheres would not be complete without your voice.

You dance in the truth that Spirit moves through you. You have something wonderful to offer life, which can only be created as you. When King David brought the Ark of the Covenant to the City of David, which to the Israelites was the ark where God was kept, David danced before the Lord with all his might. This mighty king made up his mind right then that he would tap dance, break dance, cabbage patch—clap his hands and stomp his feet—that he would gladly be a dancing fool—not just for a wooden Ark but for the Spirit that dwelled within him.

Throw away your crutches—whatever shape they may take. Get up from beside your pools of Bethesda. Touch the hem of my beloved Jesus' garment. Rise up like Lazarus. Run the race and don't get weary. Renew your course with a new strength, a new power and a new victory. There really is nothing, absolutely nothing that can hold you back. So press forward not just to win the prize but to dance—all the way to the finished line.

వ∞ళ
FROM HER SCROLL CALLED FREEDOM

I AM, she declared as if she were an affirmation.
I AM, she bellowed, as if she were an answered prayer. I AM, she
laughed, as if she was the voice of God.
I AM, she spoke, as if she was the vortex of all power. Come and look
beyond Revelation, look beyond Scripture, beyond symbols, beyond words.
When you say I AM, you call me into being
and each time I AM reborn.
వ∞ళ

Rise with a New Victory

Manna will gather her daughters from the wind,
feed their wombs with deliverance,
bless their generations with endless miracles,
shake prophecy from their mouths,
and wake victory in their midst.

෨෬

Now is the time to pull back the curtain and face the inevitable. Now is the time to cross the ultimate threshold. Now is the time. Today is the day. This is the moment that you have been waiting for—to do what you wanted to do. Chances are that you believed you had to put it off, to wait for it, to work for it, to save for it, to pray for it, or perhaps even to deserve it. But now is the time to leave your feelings of inadequacy, your feelings of lack, your feelings of doubt, your feelings of fear—and claim your victory.

Now is the time to cast the most important vote of your life—not for a president, proposition or bailout, but for the good that you can do. The fact that everything is unraveling before your eyes points to one conclusion: this is your moment. This is your time to get up off your butts and unglue yourself from whatever has been holding you back. This is your time—not just to watch the world turn, but to walk through the open door of creativity, power and strength; to become part of the solution rather than part of the problem. This is your time—not just to stand by watching "hope and change" but to become part of its mandate—by giving and receiving in a new consciousness, the true Spirit of absolute good, which has no limitation.

This is your time—not just to spew the rhetoric of peace but to really do what Thich Nhat Hanh—my beloved monk—said, to be peace in every step that you take. This is your time—not just to see the dreams of others reclaimed but to do the work that I sent each one of you to do through many lives leading to this one. There is change in the air and a hope as generous as a holy dance shouting from shore to shore and sea to shining sea. You each have the opportunity to be the change that you seek. You each have the power to do what you have been longing to do.

Remember Joshua, in the battle of Jericho? I told him not to be afraid, that I had delivered his enemies into his hands, and that not one of them would be able to withstand him. On the day when Joshua finally claimed his victory, "the sun stood still, and the moon stopped, till the nation avenged itself on its enemies."

Do not be afraid beloved: the sun has stopped in the middle of the sky and will not go down for a full day. The enlightenment before you is so intense that it is indeed a new day. After the battle of Jericho, you learn that hope was restored. The people were victorious because they had defeated their own negativity. They had stopped looking out of the eyes of their enemies, which were complacency, doubt and despair—and they began to see a world that transcended the mire of division to embrace the fellowship and stewardship of a new age. They began to see that they were the molders and shapers and builders of their lives with a new consciousness of power rather than defeat. They began an incredible new journey of transformation into the possibility of all possibilities. They awoke from the illusion that they were not accountable. They became courageous enough to become an active participant in the world. They dared to take a step out of their comfort zones to spend their remaining days sharing their gifts and talents with each other.

Take up your bed and walk—*first,* by leaving your past behind (remember, Lot's wife kept looking back and she turned into a pillar of salt); *second,* by being fully responsible for your life (no, you cannot wait for some other person or for some other time); *third,* by refusing to limit yourself (there is no limit on your happiness or success); *fourth,* by always taking the high road (you cannot conquer your challenges with the same consciousness in which you perceive them; you have to work in the spiritual realm to resolve your challenges in the physical realm); *fifth,* by becoming risk-takers (you must step outside of your comfort zones and go beyond your fears to seize the victory of something much more powerful than you could ever believe); *sixth,* by envisioning your success (all you have to do is see the end result and I will show you how to get there); and *seventh,* by opening to the divine flow (do not mock me by asking someone else what the future has in store for you; affirm what you have in store for the future). You must realize that there is nothing that you cannot do. You must become believers once again. You must be the glorious sound of the trumpet, blowing through the land without stopping—until you speak truth and find power pushing you ever so gracefully into the beauty of triumph for everyone. Then, you can finally claim your victory.

Epilogue

The finishing words come easily. The truth has already been told. It is already part of a memory. It is already in the ethers, in the wind. Now we must collect the missing scrolls.

It doesn't really matter, who came first. You are all woven from the same cloth, the same secrets, the same love. I will braid your thick soft hair today. I will put a million tiny universes in a single strand. You will finally open your eyes and see the eternal in your lasting locks and twists, rivers and streams, paths and purposes. You are sweetness and trust. You are gingersnaps and vanilla wafers. You are laughter and butterflies. You are answers and whispers.

Only my love letter could break the spell. They tried to shroud you with darkness—as something that just grew—without a mother or a father. But you have always been eternal light. Remember the stories deep in your soul. They will return to you throughout the ages. Choose the one that you will tell. A story is your soul.

The sun will shine into open windows across your bed. The trees will sway as the rays fill my heart with your radiance. Time will give birth to wonder that will embrace you with tenderness. You will feel me inside of every urging. You will feel new souls of magic and find yourself breathing me—as you.

෧❦ஓ

I Let Go

I Affirm

I See the Kingdom Within

I Tell a New Story

Once upon a time there was a brown girl named
_____and   she
was made in the image and likeness of God.

Outside of My Box, There Is

Dear God, As Me

Dear Me, As God

About the Author

In 1997, Reverend Cecilia Loving wrote a collection of poetry called *Plain Brown Girl,* which provided a framework for *Brown Girlology,* the theology underlying *God is a Brown Girl Too.* Her work embraces all women of African descent, which is the birthplace of everyone. While obtaining her Masters of Divinity from New York Theological Seminary in 2007, Rev. Loving created *Brown Girlology* and held the first God is a Brown Girl Too® Retreat in 2009 (www.godisabrowngirltoo.webs.com).

Rev. Loving was born in Detroit, Michigan but resides in Brooklyn, New York. She is the owner of Myrtle Tree Press, which has published *Prayers for Those Standing on the Edge of Greatness,* the *God is a Brown Girl Too Workbooks,* and her mother Myrtle Ross' children's books, *Angels, Angels, Everywhere* and *The Angel Blanket* (www.myrtletreepress.webs.com). She is Pastor of SPIRITMUV®, a non-denominational church in New York City (www.spiritmuv.com). Her next book, *Spiritual Fitness,* is expected to be published in 2012.

Rev. Loving also has a Juris Doctor from New York University School of Law, an M.F.A. from UCLA and a B.F.A. from Howard University. She is a member of the New York and Washington, D.C. Bars and serves as an arbitrator and mediator for several alternative dispute resolution tribunals.

She is grateful for the support of her husband Marlon Cromwell, her parents Myrtle and Hicey Ross, Raquiba LaBrie, Elizabeth Walker, Patrick Bradford, Bayliss Fiddiman, Malesha Jessie, Bianca Townsend, Rahima Wachuku, and Najah Brown.

Made in the USA
Charleston, SC
14 April 2011